COMMODORK

Thanks to Mom, Dad, and Sis for all the help, support and understanding throughout the years. Special thanks to Dad for introducing me to computers, Mom for driving me all over Oklahoma in my quest for warez, and Linda for both being my personal phone assistant and sharing a phone line with a modem all those years.

Thanks to Susan for giving me the two most beautiful children on the planet, supporting and encouraging me throughout this project, and putting up with the tons of electronic equipment I drag into our home on a regular basis.

Thanks to Arcane, The Stranger, FalseGod, Icbrkr and Phosphor Dot Fossils. Our relationships have transcended the electronic world and back. I treasure my friendships with all of you.

Special thanks to Susan and The Stranger for helping me proofread and Phosphor Dot Fossils for his assistance with the cover text.

Thanks to Kelly Rupp, Mrs. Leatherwood, Mrs. Thionnet, Koshy, Jim Smith, and every other teacher who has ever recognized my ability to write and encouraged me to continue doing so.

Thanks to all the former TBH405 crew (Rivas, Gatoperro, Anacodia, Tekin, Violetta Kitten, Yaun-Ti, Prong) along with all my friends at Digital Press, Cult of the Dead Cow, and other denizens.

Finally, thanks to all the people who called bulletin boards, ran bulletin boards, and contributed in any way to the Oklahoma City modem scene. Thank you for building the virtual world I grew up in.

Commodork: Sordid Tales from a BBS Junkie

Cover, layout, design, content and all photographs

© 2006, Rob O'Hara. All Rights Reserved.

ISBN 978-1-84728-582-9

COMMODORK:
Sordid Tales from a BBS Junkie

Rob O'Hara

"Long ago, in the time of Commodore,
There was born a word known only as "elite".
As time went by and speeds reached 14.4,
The madness took over the scene.

Chaos ruled in the land of 405,
There was no end in sight for this pain,
Users not worthy of k-rad modem jive,
Everything to lose, lameness to gain.

The Brotherhood, will live forever,
The Brotherhood, will live forever and ever."

- Flack, "The Ballad of 405" (1995)
Lyrics by Yaun-Ti

Flack in a squad car. Just playing. (2003)

Table of Contents

Interstate 405 sign, snapped during Seattle vacation (1997)

The Commodork (1987)

Chapter One

Looking Back

Something is definitely wrong with me.

For some reason, my messed-up brain attaches all my memories to physical objects. As a result of this annoying affliction I often find it difficult or impossible to throw old things away. I'm afraid that if I get rid of the things, the memories will be gone too. When I run across a childhood toy of mine (most of which I still have), I don't just see a toy; I instantly remember when and where I got it, who got it for me, and all the good times I had playing with it. My garage walls are lined with shelves, all of them sagging under the weight of toys, magazines, and books I've accumulated over the years and can't seem to part with. There is no longer enough room to park even a single a vehicle in my three-car garage. I once had a garage sale in an attempt to get rid of some of my items, but when people showed up I found it impossible to sell anything to them. A psychiatrist would no doubt have a field day with me.

I've spent the majority of my adulthood surrounding myself with the things I enjoyed as a child. My house isn't quite Pee-Wee's Playhouse yet, but I'm getting there. My backyard has a 14' x 40' building that my wife and I converted into our own arcade. It currently has twenty full size arcade games in it, as well as a slot machine, an air hockey table, and a jukebox. Most of the arcade games I own are the same games I loved playing as a kid.

Rob's Arcade (2006)

So I collect old stuff, so what? I'm not a junk collector; I don't collect junk. Six Commodore 64 computers (working or not) are not junk! You can call them retro collectables, mementos, or even spares if you wish. Just don't call them junk!

This borderline compulsive hoarding behavior wouldn't be so bad if it were limited to the garage. Unfortunately, my outside game room, my upstairs game room, and our living room entertainment center are practically bursting with DVDs, CDs, videogames, books, and toys. My Star Wars collection eventually grew so large that it had to be placed into plastic tubs and moved into the garage, where it will sit until we buy a bigger house with enough room to display it all. Our current home is almost 2,500 square feet.

Despite the fact that I'm no longer a child, I find it impossible to "put away childish things". I just have too many good memories associated with my things to let them go.

In the fall of 2005 I attended a retrogaming swap meet dubbed the Chi-Town Classic, organized by members of the popular classic videogaming website Digital Press. Thirty or so videogame aficionados from across the country meet one Saturday morning each year in a videogame store owned by one of the board's forum members. While the store (Videogames, Etc.) is located near Chicago's O'Hare Airport, people came from as far away as New Jersey to attend the event. I myself drove 800 miles (each way) just to attend. Attendants brought stacks of plastic tubs full of old videogame-related paraphernalia to sell and trade. It's a neat event to attend, even if you aren't in the market to buy anything. I personally spent hours looking through each person's piles, smiling each time I found an item that reminded me of my youth. When I spied a pair of wireless Atari 2600 joysticks (still in the box), I was instantly taken back to elementary school, when my father brought home a pair of the exact same joysticks so that he and I could sit all the way across the living room from our big screen television and play River Raid on the Atari 2600.

As the day went on the storefront windows continued magnifying the afternoon sun, further raising the temperature in a room already a bit warm from too many bodies. One of the attendees came up with the idea to prop open the store's front door to allow a breeze to flow in, and once this was done the room began to cool off. A few minutes later when I walked from the back of the store up to the front, I literally gasped at what I saw. Someone had used a Commodore 64 to prop the store's front door open!

Now you must understand that whenever I see a Commodore 64 computer, I don't see an outdated hunk of computing plastic, barely powerful enough to balance one's checkbook on these days. Every time I see one I'm instantly taken back to all the great adventures I had over the years with my own Commodore system. My mind floods with memories of the people I met, the games I played, the trouble I got into and the bulletin board systems I called. This particular one had the words "UNTESTED/UNKNOWN" written on the bottom of it in typical thrift-store handwriting, next to the unit's selling price: $2.98. But I didn't see a 25-year-old chunk of plastic that most likely didn't even work. I saw a decade's worth of good memories, sitting out there on the sidewalk.

Throughout the day I made it a point to keep an eye on that little computer. For a while I looked for something to replace it with, but I was forced to eventually accept the fact that the machine's slightly sloped shape did indeed make for a perfectly ergonomic doorstop. I constantly worried that someone might steal it off the open sidewalk. (Keep in mind that we're talking about a potentially broken $3 computer here.) Later in the day I began to secretly hope that someone actually *would* steal it in an attempt to liberate the machine from door-propping slavery.

Soon it was night, and attendees of the swap fest began to pack up their items and leave. One by one people carried mountains of archaic plastic and circuit boards out of the store, stuffing them into awaiting vehicles. No one stopped to rescue that poor Commodore 64 computer. After almost everyone had left, I began asking around. "Hey, do you know whose Commodore 64 that is? I think someone forgot to pick it up!" But the more I asked, the more I realized that no one else was particularly concerned about the machine or its well being. Maybe they had never owned one, or if they did maybe they just saw the battered piece of junk sitting on the sidewalk for what it really was: old, abused, and most likely lifeless.

But not me.

With but a few people remaining in the store, I announced my departure. On the way out of the store I bent over and picked the little feller up off the sidewalk.

"I'M TAKING THIS HOME!" I announced. No one objected; a few people even laughed. With that declaration I tucked the machine under my arm and walked out of the store. The door, finally admitting defeat, swung shut behind me.

When I arrived home a few days later from my Chicago adventure, I snuck my newly acquired Commodore into the house. While I thought my wife was distracted I pulled the beige machine out from deep within my suitcase and crept out to the garage to store it. My wife, suspecting I was up to something, quietly followed me out to the garage where she caught me red handed.

"Dear God, not another one," she said, only half joking.

On one set of shelves in my garage sit stacks of old computers, partial computers, and computer parts. One shelf is completely dedicated to Commodore computers. Half a dozen spare Commodore disk drives are stacked on one end of the shelf, while just as many actual Commodore computers sit at the other end. Why I continue to buy them, I'm not sure. Sometimes I tell people that I buy them as spares in case the one I currently use breaks down. "You can't just go into a store and buy one of these things new anymore you know," I'll tell them. The statement itself has little to no merit; the Commodore 64 I used extensively throughout the 1980s still works fine. I'm not sure what the life expectancy of one of these computers is or if they even have one. And even if they *do* have one the machine I'm currently using has been working for 25 years now – at that rate I have enough spare Commodore computers to get me through at least the next two centuries.

The real reason I buy them is because when I run across them in the wild, whether it's in the bottom of a thrift store bin or on the sidewalk being used as a doorstop, they look sad to me. I think of all the great times I had on those machines and I think someone else could use one and possibly have fun with it as well. I also always think what a good bargain they are, comparing their current selling price to the price they originally sold for twenty years ago. The problem is, I can never seem to find anyone to give all these adopted machines to, and when I do find someone I typically find a reason not to part with them. So, out in the garage they sit.

See? I told you something was definitely wrong with me.

Of all the arcade cabinets, videogame systems, retro computer systems and mountains of games I own, my original Commodore 64 computer is still probably my most prized possession. Purchased back in 1985 and still kicking, it's currently hooked up in my computer room next to machines twenty years newer. Every now and then I'll break out my huge green milk crate full of old floppy disks and thumb through them. The milk crate is filled to the top with close to a thousand 5 ¼" floppies, each one numbered and labeled by my own hands many years ago. Some of them are over two decades old now. Even though it's been a long time, just by looking at the labels I can often remember where I got a particular game from, or with whom I used to play it. The disk with "Bard's Tale" handwritten in black marker on its browning, peeling label sits on top of the stack. As I run my finger across the label, I think of the summer my friend Charon and I spent playing the game. The two of us spent much of the summer of '86 huddled in front of his computer, eating cold pizza and cheese puffs and each drinking Dr. Pepper straight out of three-liter bottles. Each weekend we'd huddle in front of his monitor, playing deep into the night until I would begin to fall asleep around two or three in the morning. When I would wake up around eight or nine in the morning, Charon would still be playing. From the bed I could see images of the game reflected in his glasses. Then a changing of the guard would take place – after a quick debriefing of the night's discoveries, he would go to sleep and I would take over our party's destiny. By the end of that summer I knew the streets and back alleys of Skara Brae (the mythical town Bard's Tale takes place in) better than I knew my own neighborhood.

Every diskette in the stack has a unique number and a unique memory associated with it.

When I see my old Newsroom diskettes I remember the time a buddy of mine and I were going to start our own school newspaper. My old C-Net BBS disks remind me of the hundreds of hours Arcane and I spent talking on the phone late at night, modifying our boards' code and pushing our poor computers to the breaking point.

In 1993 I retired my Commodore computer (for the first time) and purchased an IBM 386 DX/40, using money my future mother-in-law gave my then girlfriend (now wife) to pay for her college tuition. By then the Commodore 64 was all but obsolete, surpassed in speed and power by 16-bit gaming consoles such as the Super Nintendo and Sega Genesis. Without an affordable hard drive or any real upgrade options, the C64 was bypassed in the business world as well by the new generation of powerful (and upgradeable) IBM PCs and Macintoshes.

Most of the memories I associate with my old computer collection go back to my old local modem scene. It both surprises and amazes me that more effort has not gone into documenting the BBS era. During the golden age of bulletin boards (from the early 1980s through the mid-1990s), the modem world *was* our Internet. It was the way we talked to other computer users, traded programs and met people. The technology behind bulletin boards may seem archaic today – computers talking to each other one at a time at painfully slow speeds over dial up phone lines – but to those of us who lived it, it was an incredible, magical time. It was cutting edge technology that we got to play with every day. For many years the modem world *was* my world, and a major part of my reality.

I quite literally grew up behind a keyboard. I met my first girlfriend online. I drank my first beer at a modem party. Most of my best friends in real life have been people I first encountered online virtually. Beginning at age ten, my primary entertainment, conversation and socialization was delivered to me through a phone line connected to a computer.

A few of my old Commodore diskettes (2006)

My Commodore diskettes have been through a lot.

Recently, I've noticed that some of my old floppy disks have begun to fade from existence. Some have started losing their labels, retaining only a small patch of sticky-goo where the disk's label was once affixed. Some may have had their data cooked by being stored in my garage during one too many scorching Oklahoma summers. Most of them are simply reaching the end of their life expectancy. I'm not sure anyone intended for these floppies to last into the new millennium. The disks are deteriorating both physically and electronically. The most upsetting part of their decline is that I've noticed as the disks have begun fade, so have my memories. Sometimes I'll start telling one of my old computer tales only to realize I don't remember how it ended. Occasionally I'll get halfway through a story and start questioning whether I've included the right people or places in the tale. I recently ran across an old spiral notebook of mine filled with computer-related notes written in my own handwriting that made absolutely no sense to me at all. None of the notes, names, numbers or passwords looked even remotely familiar. Without these disks around to jog my brain, I know that when they are gone the stories and history of that era will disappear as well.

It would be impossible to document the entire BBS experience (although Jason Scott has done an admirable job trying with his BBS Documentary DVDs). Every single bulletin board that existed was a unique identity. Unlike the Internet, for the most part bulletin boards were not networked together. Each and every BBS was its own independent island of information, complete with its own users and conversations. Since users tended to call bulletin boards inside their own local area code (to avoid long distance phone charges), each area code had its own pocket of boards and users who existed only within their own little microcosm.

Along with its own user base, every BBS had its own unique set up, configuration, graphics, look, feel, and content. Like teenagers with their first car, sysops (system operators, the people who ran bulletin boards) spent many hours modifying and customizing their systems, making each one unique. And when these bulletin boards were finally powered off for the last time, the historical records of everything that took place throughout the years on them vanished from existence. Very little of the data was backed up or archived. Most of the stories and adventures that took place during that time were not documented. Even more frustrating was the fact that you rarely got notice that a BBS was about to go offline. One day a board would be there, and the next time you called instead of hearing a modem you might instead get three loud tones blasting through your speaker followed by a familiar and disappointing message: "We're sorry, but the number you have dialed has been disconnected or is no longer in service …"

And eventually, the entire modem community ceased to exist. In the mid 1990s the arrival of the Internet crushed the modem world into oblivion, making BBSes obsolete almost overnight.

If each area code had its own modem scene, I'll bet you are wondering why on earth you should care about mine. The fact is that while the details of all of our computer backgrounds may be different, I guarantee you will find things within this book you can relate to. Regardless of the specific type of computer you may have owned, all of us who were there have similar memories of "those days." Simply being a computer owner back in the 1980s is enough to induct you into an honorary timeless club. Even if the details are different we all have common stories, memories and milestones. We all remember the first time we saw a personal computer, and what got us hooked. We all remember typing in our first program, the first time we were able to make a computer do something we instructed it to do. We all remember playing our favorite games. We all remember the thrill of connecting a phone line to our computer and calling someone else's computer for the first time. And, for those of us who were sysops, we all remember the thrill of someone else calling *our* computer for the first time. We all remember how big our first hard drives were and how much we paid for them. So even though the stories within this book come from my own personal experiences, I am sure you will find familiar themes that you will be able to relate with and enjoy

I also think those who were not around during this exciting era will get a kick out of the adventures retold here. As I was explaining the focus of this book to a co-worker (a much younger computer tech), he informed me that he had never called a BBS and had only "heard about them" as if they were some long lost, mystical thing. Believe it or not, there *was* life before the Internet! Most of these stories don't even seem very old to me! And yet, those same memories and stories that took place only a few years ago seem to be quickly fading. I hope that by telling the small story of one area code, it will somehow relate to the bigger story of BBSes in every area code.

That is my motivation here: to share classic stories to those who were there, to entertain and educate those who were not, and most importantly to preserve the stories, experiences and great memories I have of some of the best years of my life, growing up online.

The stories contained within this book are, to the best of my knowledge and memory, 100% true. Every tale contained within this tome is an experience that I myself witnessed firsthand. However, everything contained within has also been stored in my cluttered brain for some time now before being regurgitated here. Hopefully, I've remembered the majority of the details correctly. As I previously stated, there are few (if any) written accounts existing that document the majority of these events. Therefore, most of the dates found within this book should be considered little more than educated guesses. Likewise, every story printed between these covers is told from my personal point of view. I've tried to be as impartial and factual as possible, but keep in mind that some of the memories are beginning to fade along with those old diskettes. When possible I've consulted old friends to confirm dates and facts, but the more I did this the more I realized that often two faulty memories aren't much better than one.

One decision I made early on during the writing of this book was to refer to the people mentioned within by their online aliases instead of their real names. I hope that by doing so you'll understand just how closely my online and real lives were interwoven. My friends and I often referred to one another by our handles on a regular basis. Many people I met over the years thought that "Jack Flack" was my given name, and in certain circles I was addressed as "Jack" or "Flack" more so than by my real name. It was not uncommon for my mother to answer the phone, cover the mouthpiece and shout, "phone call for Jack Flack!"

A final caveat before beginning our adventure: piracy is bad. We know that now. In the early days, we didn't know, and when we found out, we didn't care. Our parents didn't care and the police didn't care either. In fact the only people who actually cared about piracy were the people writing and/or selling software, and nobody cared that *they* cared. Back then we didn't have the World Wide Web; we had the Wild Wild West.

Today life is different. I pay for the software I need, the music I listen to and the services I use. But this book isn't about now. It's about a time where pirated software ruled the land. Those with the most, newest, and best programs had the power; those who didn't groveled at their feet. It's about good friends, good times, good memories, and good warez.

And to think, it all started with two blocky paddles hitting a blocky square back and forth across our television screen.

Chapter Two

Old School

My earliest videogame-related memory is of playing Pong in my parent's living room at the age of four. It was Thanksgiving Day, 1977, and I remember that my aunt, uncle and two cousins had come over to join us for a big Thanksgiving Day meal. To a four-year-old kid, the most important thing about Thanksgiving is (or at least was) watching the Thanksgiving Day Parade. You got to see floats, you got to see huge balloons, and at the end of the parade you got to see Santa Claus usher in the Christmas season. Back then the Christmas season officially began the weekend after Thanksgiving, not two weeks before Halloween like it does now.

That November afternoon, my dad had a surprise for our family: Pong. Despite my single dissenting vote to wait for Santa's appearance, the parade was switched off and Pong was turned on. Along with Pong, our unit also played Soccer, Tennis, and Squash, all of which were basic variations of Pong. "That thing will play any game in the world ... as long as it's Pong," my dad used to say. While the idea of Pong may not seem very groundbreaking to you today, being able to hold something in your hand that interacted with your own television seemed quite amazing back then.

For those too young to remember, I'm sure old television commercials and print advertisements that showed entire families huddled around the living room television staring at primitive-looking games must seem bizarre or even hilarious, but I promise you that's exactly how I remember it. There we were – eight of us in all, gathered around the television and watching a square dot bounce back and forth, as bewildered and excited as cavemen must've been the day they discovered fire.

And I guess that day we really did discover fire, or at least I did. The flame I hold for videogames that burns today can be traced back to that very day. That flame has evolved into the hobby and the passion that I continue to enjoy today, which in itself contains two traits I've inherited from my parents: my father's love of all things electronic, and my mother's inability to throw anything away. Yes, somewhere, we still have that same Pong unit our family purchased back in 1977.

For thirty years my father worked at Oklahoma Graphics, a large printing company based in Oklahoma City. As a foreman, he was required to put in overtime hours on a weekly basis. All those extra hours worked throughout the year translated to a sizable tax refund check every spring, which always went toward purchasing one large entertainment-related item for the entire family to enjoy. Since the cash was technically my father's, the purchased item was usually technical in nature. For example, in the spring of 1978 we got our first VCR and video camera, one of the first ones in town. The two items combined cost over $1,000. The VCR was one of the first able to record at both two-hour *and* four-hour speeds! I can remember the buttons being so stiff that I had to use both thumbs to press them down. The camera recorded in black and white only and had to be connected to the VCR at all times with a long cable. Every Christmas and birthday for years to come, my parents would set the camera up on a tripod and place it in a corner of the living room to record the present-opening festivities. My birthday parties were the largest in the neighborhood, as kids from blocks away would bring a gift over just for the opportunity to see themselves on television.

Later that same year, dad also bought our family Magnavox's brand new videogame console, the Odyssey II – there must've been some refund money left over. Released a year after the Atari 2600, the Odyssey II also sported a keyboard that made it look more like a computer than a gaming console. According to my father he picked the Odyssey II over the Atari 2600 because of its superior graphics, but despite the system's apparent technical superiority games were nearly impossible to find. Either stores didn't stock them, or were constantly sold out of them. After getting fed up of never being able to find games for the system, dad boxed the entire thing up, stuck it in the closet (yeah, I still have that one too), and purchased an Atari 2600.

From the summer of 1978 through the summer of 1980, the Atari 2600 became *the* standard gaming console of choice. It seems like everybody had an Atari back then, and the few kids that didn't quickly made friends with somebody who did. Again, compared to modern videogame systems it may be difficult to understand just how amazing the Atari was, despite the machine's simplistic technical abilities. We played even the most basic games like Basketball, Bowling and Combat for hours at a time. And when companies began porting arcade games over to the Atari, things got even *more* exciting! The day Space Invaders came out, my dad let me skip school so the two of us could go down to Toys-R-Us and purchase it together. The excitement generated by Space Invaders was nothing compared to the release of Pac-Man just a few years later. Pac-Man for the Atari 2600 has been cited by many as the most disappointing game ever released and one of the causes of the great videogame crash of 1983, but at the time we were thrilled to have a version of Pac-Man we could play in our homes. So what if it didn't look as good as the arcade version? What game on the Atari 2600 did?

Even though Atari games often came with dozens of options and possible configurations, that wasn't enough for my circle of friends. So, we began inventing our own ways of playing them. We often held contests to see who could get the highest score on Video Pinball with their eyes closed or who could get the furthest in Pac-Man while holding the joystick upside down. Even on a system that we couldn't program for, we were creating our own games. This need to create and do something new and original with games would not fully begin to be realized until the summer of 1980.

On New Year's Eve, 1979, our neighbors (the Simers) invited my family over to proudly show us their newest purchase: a HOME COMPUTER! Sitting on a desk in the back of their den was the first computer I ever saw in person, a Radio Shack TRS-80 Model I. My father and I stood behind Mr. Simer as he showed us the awesome processing power his 4K machine harnessed. He had also purchased the (apparently somewhat rare) Voice Synthesizer Module, and we laughed as Mr. Simer typed in four-letter words (that I didn't know the meaning of at the time) and made the computer recite them back to us using its quirky, synthesized voice. Mr. Simer also showed us a car racing game written completely in BASIC. The car looked like this: ":0:" and the sides of the road were drawn with |, / and \ characters. I remember steering the car down the road using the keyboard's arrow keys, and I don't think you were able to control the car's speed at all. Today you couldn't get a kid to play that crappy game for ten seconds even on their cell phone out in the desert, but back then it seemed pretty amazing.

Before we left the Simers' house that evening I knew that we would soon own a home computer. It only took dad a couple of days to make his decision. When my father marched down to Radio Shack to purchase our own TRS-80 Model I, the salesman at the store informed us that the model III would be released later that spring. To be honest I don't remember if my dad paid a down payment or not, but I do remember Radio Shack putting our name down on a waiting list, guaranteeing us the first TRS-80 Model III to arrive in Yukon, Oklahoma. Later that year we got the phone call we had been waiting for; the computer had arrived. When we walked into Radio Shack, we found the box had already been opened. Immediately, the salesmen apologized to us.

"We're sorry we opened the box," one of them said. "We just wanted to see one in person! We've never seen one of these before!"

With that purchase, we became elite members of the "Personal Computer Owners Club". Our Model III had two plastic plates covering where the optional disk drives could have gone. Dual disk drives were, I believe, a $1,000 option. Instead of disk drives we got the data cassette recorder. Using the same cassettes that a home stereo used, programs could be easily (but not speedily) saved and loaded.

The term "slow" has always been used when describing computers, but to me there are two different kinds of slow. First off, there's the "slow" that is only apparent when in comparison to something faster. For example, the Pentium 60 is slow compared to modern computers, but compared to our TRS-80 Model III it would seem blazingly fast! But then there's the kind of slow that, when you see it, you know it's slow. There is no comparison needed with anything past, present or future to fully comprehend its slowness. That's the kind of slow the TRS-80 Model III's cassette tape drive operated at: *maximus slowiness*. In an age filled with things measured in nanoseconds it seems unfathomably slow, but no one in the history of computing has ever described Tandy's cassette drive as fast. Not now, not then. It was slow. And in order to save a thousand dollars, we dealt with it.

One of the first games I remember playing on our computer was a text adventure named Haunted House. Haunted House took over 15 minutes to load from cassette, and that was just for the *first* half of the game! The second half resided on the flip side of the cassette, which meant after playing through the first half of the game you had to flip the cassette over and load the second half for another fifteen minutes. Hey, there's only so much you could do with 4k of RAM. (Incidentally, my current cell phone has 128 Meg of RAM and another gig of storage.) If you got killed during the second half of the game, there was no way to simply continue. You had to reload the first half of the game all over again.

Text adventures were the first genre of games I remember becoming really popular in the home computer market. Computer graphics at the time were extremely primitive, but text adventures were essentially like interactive books where all the "graphics" took place in your mind. All of them were essentially the same in structure. When the game began, there would be a short introductory paragraph, explaining who you were and what your ultimate goal was. Underneath that would be a short paragraph describing where you were, obvious directions you could travel, and any objects you could see. For example, a pirate-themed game might begin with, "You are standing on the deck of a large pirate ship. You can go NORTH, EAST, or WEST from here. There is a rusty sword lying on the deck in front of you." For many years, most text adventures used simple two word parsers, so your first command might have been "GET SWORD" at which point the game might have informed you, "You have successfully taken the sword." If you typed the word INVENTORY and hit enter, the game would give you a list of items you were carrying. "You are now carrying a rusty sword."

Scott Adams, unrelated to the Dilbert author of the same name, was the king of text adventures. His game *Adventureland* was the first text adventure designed to run on a home computer instead of a mainframe. *Adventureland* was one of twelve adventure games included in the Scott Adams Gold Collection, which included such classics as *The Count*, *Voodoo Castle*, and *Mystery Fun House*. My dad and I enjoyed his games so much that at one point we joined the Scott Adams Fan Club and received an autographed picture of Scott (sitting with his arm around an airbrushed monster) mailed to us.

SPECIAL GOLD EDITION

Scott Adams and "Friend" (1980?)

There were three main reasons that text adventures became popular. The first reason was that the TRS-80's graphical ability sucked. Its integrated 12-inch black and white monitor could only display 16 lines of 64 characters, and graphically impressed no one. The second reason, and the reason this hobby was so much fun for so many years, was because for the most part smart people owned computers. Nobody's grandmother owned a TRS-80 Model III. Nobody sat around mindlessly playing Solitaire all day long back then. Nobody's computer collected dust. Back then, people who owned computers wanted them. Badly. And the majority of those people were people with an above average intelligence who liked to read. The third reason text adventures were popular is pretty simple: other than a few BASIC games that relied on ASCII numbers and letters for their graphics, they didn't have much competition.

Many of the programs we had on our TRS-80 we typed in by hand ourselves. Computer magazines of the time would include the source code of BASIC programs that users could type in. They almost never worked the first time. "SYNTAX ERROR IN LINE 10," the computer would say while rejecting your program. Then the manual troubleshooting process of comparing each line in the program with each line printed in the magazine would begin. Keep in mind that some of these programs had hundreds or even thousands of lines in them. And sometimes, after checking every single line, the programs still wouldn't run. In that case you would have to wait until the following month's magazine came out and see if any corrections had been included. It was a frustrating process, but it was a cheap (and sometimes the only) way to get new software.

And speaking of software, I remember going with my dad many times to Radio Shack to look at all the available games. I remember each game having fantastic artwork on the cover. One space game had a fantastic painting of a space ship flying past a planet, but when we got the game home the instructions read something like, "you are the white triangle. Avoid the white dot." It certainly didn't seem very fair. In fact it seemed a lot like false advertising to me.

One of my favorite TRS-80 stories happened to me in second grade. One day during recess I told a fellow classmate that I had a computer at home. That kid told another kid, who told the teacher about my claims. The teacher proceeded to give me a lecture about lying and told me how important it was to always tell the truth! Keep in mind that in 1980 telling someone you had a computer at your house was a lot like telling people you had eaten lunch on the moon the day before. When I told my dad about the incident, he backed me up. The next day, my dad brought our home computer up to our school, along with our dot matrix printer. We had a program at the time that would generate and print out word searches after entering in a list of words into the computer. Dad made a word search with all my classmates' names in it and printed out enough copies for everybody to have one. It was such a big event that even our principal came down to our classroom to check out our computer.

From 1980 to 1983, the TRS-80 Model III and the Atari 2600 lived hand in hand in my world. While other neighborhood kids were out playing baseball, I wrote a program to compute batting statistics. I wrote a calculator program to help me do my math homework. I even wrote a simple program that would quiz you on your dinosaur knowledge. When I wasn't sitting in front of the computer, I was sitting in front of the television playing Atari 2600 games like Pitfall, Laser Blast, and Keystone Kapers. Between the TRS-80 Model III computer and the Atari 2600 gaming system, my world could not have been any better.

And then the Apple II computer was released, which redefined what my world was.

Rob with sister Linda (1979)

Chapter Three

Apples

While my favorite computer of all time is indisputably the Commodore 64, if it hadn't been for Apple computers I might have lost interest in the hobby before ever seeing my first Commodore. If the TRS-80 Model III was kindergarten, the Apple II was grade school. From hustling warez to surviving in the BBS world, everything I would later perfect in the Commodore and IBM PC realms I learned on the Apple – which was odd because technically we didn't even own an Apple computer; we owned a Franklin Ace 1000, an Apple II clone.

Even though the Apple II was originally released in 1977, not only did I not know anyone who owned one back then, I didn't know anyone who knew anyone who knew anyone who owned one back then. It wasn't until the Apple IIe was released in 1982 that Apples began appearing in public places. By 1983 you could get an Apple IIe for $1395 (the 100% Apple compatible Franklin Ace 1000 cost just under a grand). As far as the personal computer market was concerned, the writing was on the wall for Tandy. As Apple began donating thousands of computers to public schools across the country, the TRS-80 was out and the Apple II was in. During that same time my dad had been considering installing dual floppy disk drives into our TRS-80, the price of which had dropped to around $700. Instead, he sold the TRS-80 for $300, combined that money with the money he had been saving for the disk drives, and brought home our new "Apple", the Franklin Ace 1000. (For the record, the Franklin Ace 1000 was a little too similar to the Apple IIe . Apple sued Franklin for copyright infringement over the similarities between the two machines and won.)

The technological gap between the TRS-80 and the Apple was quite significant. Apple computers had more than a few features our TRS-80 Model III lacked, including color, and graphics, and real sound, and disk drives, and a joystick, and most importantly to this book, a modem.

Modems of the early 1980s were basically identical to the modems of today, except of course they operated at much slower speeds. In 1981 Hayes released the Smartmodem, which allowed computers to talk directly to modems (this replaced acoustic coupler modems, the old modems that required users to physically place their telephone's handset on in order to operate). In the early days, 300 baud modems ran anywhere from $200-$400 depending on the manufacturer, while 1200 baud modems (the next step up) could cost up to a thousand dollars. Like everything else in the computer world, modem prices dropped every time a newer, faster product was released.

Our computer's modem introduced my dad and me along with an entire generation of technogeeks to the brand new world of online computing. Back then there were no Internet Service Providers, online services or anything of that nature. Modems were used to call Bulletin Board Systems (often referred to as BBSes or simply boards for short) run by sysops. For the record, the word "sysop" is most definitely pronounced "siss-awp" and not "sEYE-sawp", which a few defiant dorks insisted on using. And while I'm on the subject, "warez" is pronounced "where's," not "ware-EZ." Oddly enough, modem (which everyone agrees on how to pronounce) is a combination of the words MOdulate/DEModulate, which means technically we all pronounce that one wrong. Oh well, nerds will be nerds.

Most bulletin boards were run by sysops out of their homes on their own hardware. Running a board wasn't cheap – the first BBSes predated multitasking, so running one meant purchasing at a minimum a computer (a thousand dollar investment) dedicated to running the board 24/7, along with an additional dedicated phone line for another thirty to forty dollars a month.

Most bulletin boards fell under one of three categories. Some boards were set up mainly as message boards, others were set up for playing online games, and the rest were set up for trading software. It was not uncommon for a BBS to provide all three of those services, but most boards catered to one more than the other two – boards with active file areas usually had message boards filled with pointless drivel, and vice versa.

Online games were a huge trend that I never really got into. There were many of them around, all of them turn based and all of them (at least it seemed to me) loosely based on the board game Risk. Callers were allowed a limited amount of moves per day, and they moved much too slowly to hold my interest. The biggest problem with these games was that if a game on a particular board got popular, players would keep a system busy all day long and no one else could dial in, making for dead message and file areas.

The good news is, there were plenty of other boards around to call, so it didn't matter much. Before long I had accounts on fifty or sixty different Apple bulletin boards, and the terminal program I used would go down the list dialing boards in order until it eventually connected to one. Through message boards I began making friends with dozens of people all across the city, and through file areas I began, well, trading files.

VisiCalc was the first electronic spreadsheet developed for personal computers. It made Apple computers fly off the shelf, escalated home computers from being toys to viable business machines, and is considered to be one of the most revolutionary programs of all time. And, as a nine-year-old kid, I couldn't have cared less. At that time I only cared about one thing: GAMES. Finally, gone were the BASIC, text-only programs from the TRS-80. The Apple had real games, games I had heard of before like Pac-Man and Donkey Kong. And, they were all free!

They were free, of course, because we stole them. Games were there for the taking, so we took them. Piracy is the act of making illegal copies of software. Back then it was covered under the same copyright laws as making copies out of a book at your local public library, or dubbing a cassette tape off a friend's. I cannot stress strongly enough what a big deal it *wasn't* in those days. I traded software with police officers, preacher's kids and schoolteachers on a regular basis. It wasn't like it is today, where people go to jail for piracy. Computer piracy was as serious as recording a song off the radio, and the odds of getting arrested for either one were about the same.

In the TRS-80 days, piracy wasn't much of a problem. Part of that was because of the cassette media we used. No one traded cassette tapes on any sort of mass scale – the logistics and time involved of such a practice prevented it. And even if we had wanted to, we only knew about three other people with computers. But Apple computers were different. They had quickly invaded businesses, schools, and homes. Not everyone you knew had a computer, but most people knew someone who did, and that was quite a change.

Our Apple had two disk drives, which only served one real purpose: to expedite and simplify the act of copying software. Copying games using only one disk drive involved swapping multiple times between the original (the source) and a blank disk (the target), as the Apple didn't have enough RAM to store the entire contents of a diskette in its memory. To be quite frank, copying games using only one drive was a pain in the ass. It was slow, tedious, and prone to errors. More than one original game diskette was accidentally overwritten and ruined by inserting the wrong disk at the wrong time.

Having dual disk drives came to your advantage when it came time for what I called "copy negotiations". There were only two ways for acquaintances to trade software back then: you could transfer software over the phone lines using your modem, or you could physically go to a person's house and trade games in person (which was actually much more time efficient). Trading games over the modem was slow – a single game might take a couple of hours to transfer at 300 baud. In the same amount of time you could just drive to the person's house, copy an entire box-load of games, and drive back home, which is often what we did.

Sooner or later the decision had to be made as to who was doing the driving. That's where those copy negotiations came into play. Having dual disk drives helped, as you would be able to copy games much faster than someone else who only had one drive, but the best negotiating tool a person could possess was software. The more you had, the more control you had over the situation. If you had twice as many games as the person you were trading with, you could practically force them to come to you instead of the other way around. This was why everyone collected "trade-bait" in addition to the games we actually wanted to play. Trade-bait was simply software that you collected for the sole purpose of using to trade with other people down the line. I'm pretty sure that's why my dad had a copy of the Bible for the computer. While I highly doubt anyone in my family ever gathered around the green glow of a computer monitor to read Holy Scriptures, the next guy you met might be looking for it (and be holding the very game you were looking for).

I began to learn how "the warez game" worked by watching my father. Dad would meet people through his work, computer user groups or simply online and set up trades with them. Regardless of whether the trading took place at their place or ours, I was always there by his side. Some of these guys may have thought my dad was forcing me to tag along, but in reality there was no place I would have rather been! Sometimes the trades wouldn't be very fruitful and we might only get one or two new programs. One time my dad and I went to a guy's house (a mobile home), and when we got there all the guy had to offer us was a bunch of crappy public domain software. Over time, we got better at finding out what specific programs people had before committing to a drive across the city. Sometimes, things would work out great and we would find people with seemingly unlimited amounts of software. Those were the contacts you treated well and hung on to dearly. One of those people was a guy named Mertz.

Mertz was a college student. To me (a ten-year-old kid) he seemed like the coolest dude ever, an older guy who lived for computers and would trade with us. Mertz lived just off campus in a small two-room apartment. One room was his bedroom, while the other housed his rather massive computer collection. Mertz ran one of the largest Apple pirate bulletin boards in the area at that time. I'm not sure how my father hooked up with him but he did, and since Mertz had the goods, we would load up our boxes of games on a monthly basis and make the half-hour drive to the guy's house to trade software.

Mertz's computer room, which started out as a small bedroom, had less free floor space than most closets. One wall was covered floor to ceiling in shelves, which were themselves overflowing with disks, manuals and computer parts. The other side of the room had a couple of computer desks that not only had Apple computers but also disks, manuals and computer parts. What floor space was left had two beat up office chairs that were surrounded by disks, manuals, and computer parts. The whole room looked like a mad scientist's lab shortly after an explosion.

Since there was only room for two people in the computer room, I often sat just outside in the living room while the two of them traded software back and forth. Like many other college students, Mertz played a lot of role-playing games during that time, and while I waited in the living room I would entertain myself by flipping through his Dungeons and Dragons monster manuals and other related literature. I didn't mind waiting, knowing that when we got home I would have dozens of new games to play. Dad and Mertz became good friends and did quite a bit of software trading over the years. His BBS was one of the busiest in the area, and the amount of new software he got on a daily basis was astounding. It was embarrassing how little we had to offer the guy in return, but he always seemed to enjoy our visits and my dad would often offer him blank disks for free as a token of our appreciation.

I remember thinking at the time I couldn't wait to go to college so I could live like Mertz.

One difference between copying software and buying software is that when you buy software, you also get the instructions – not so with pirated programs. But, there were ways around that too.

My dad worked out a pretty good technique for figuring out how to play most games. Once a game had started, dad would press his arm down on one edge of the keyboard and begin sliding it across the keys. The minute anything happened in the program, he would move him arm back and forth and narrow down exactly which key did what. He would continue this process until he had mapped out the entire keyboard, and would then write his findings up into a text file. Those documentation files were known as docs, or "dox" for short. Writing dox was a good way to get your name out into trading circles, as they were sometimes as valuable as the games themselves were.

A lot of games came with "code wheels", which were little paper disks that, when lined up properly, would reveal the correct password needed to start a game. Did I mention my dad worked at a printing press? Code wheels were quite easily defeated by your average Xerox copier. Simply disassemble, copy, and reassemble.

And, when all else failed, I would borrow the instruction manuals from a friend who had purchased a game, and copy it by hand. If it was good enough for monks, it was good enough for me.

To get started in software trading circles, you really only needed one source. Once you had a few games, you could trade those games with someone else to get copies of their new games. You could repeat this process as often and with as many people as you wanted to. One problem with trading software was once you had given out a program, you needed to get as many trades out of it as possible. If you waited a day, the person to whom you gave a copy to may have already traded the game with other people you traded with! I can remember setting up multiple trades with multiple people using the same game and then making all the trades as quickly as possible, in order to get the maximum mileage out of a hot new program.

If all of this sounds like a big game, that's because it was. While there was no official scorekeeping, the people who played the game right were the ones who ended up with the newest, best, and largest piles of software. More importantly, those who weren't any good at playing the game ended up at the mercy to those who were.

Of course, it wasn't just about collecting games – it was also about playing them! One of the earliest Apple games I really remember my dad and I both getting into was Wizardry. Wizardry was the first "dungeon crawler" we had ever seen, and was the first Dungeons and Dragons-style game to contain hi-res graphics. At first, my dad and I each created our own party, but we soon realized we could get further in the game if we both played using the same group – that way, we could advance our characters twice as fast. At that point in time my dad was working weekdays from 3-11 pm. Each day when I got home from school I would fire up Wizardry and pick up where my father had left off the night before. My dad used to bring home huge sheets of graph paper from his work, on which we would map out the different dungeons and mark down treasures and monsters, traps we had discovered, and puzzles we had solved. I would play for a few hours each night, updating the notes my father had left me the night before. Each night after work he'd come in, take a shower, sit down at the computer and begin the cycle all over again. The system was similar to the one my friend Charon and I would use to beat Bard's Tale, another dungeon crawler, just a few years later.

Things really began to take off in Wizardry once I came up with a copy of WizFix, a program that allowed you to manually edit your characters and create God-like warriors. How I ended up with a copy of WizFix is an interesting story.

Doug, the kid who lived next door to me, was a year older than me. His older brother Greg was into everything we thought was cool at the time: ninjas, heavy metal, and Dungeons and Dragons. About once a week Greg would have the "older" kids from the neighborhood over to play Dungeons and Dragons in his family's "back garage", a detached two-car garage that had a big pool table in the middle of it which doubled as a poker table, domino table, and Dungeons and Dragons playfield as needed. We younger kids weren't allowed to play of course, so we would simply stand around on the weekends watching the big kids play. One of the kids that regularly attended these weekly D&D parties was a teenager named Shannon.

Shannon was into the same stuff as the rest of us, but he was also really into Apple computers. Once or twice he had even invited me over to his house to check out the setup in his room, which consisted of library tables pressed against all four walls, each one covered in multiple layers of computer disks and magazines. A mattress lay pushed up against one of the walls under one of the tables, presumably where Shannon would sleep after hacking around on his Apple late into the night. One of the few times I was invited to his house, I noticed that Shannon had a copy of Wizardry too. When I asked him if he played much, he loaded the game up and showed me his party. When I saw his characters, I couldn't believe it! Where my fighters were level 3, his were level 300! And not only that, he had character classes I had never even seen before. His fighters were samurai; his thieves were ninjas. I had never seen anything like it before! When I asked him how he had got so far in the game, he slyly replied, "I'll never tell." After persistent begging, Shannon said he would tell me how he did it in a couple of weeks.

One day shortly after our visit, Shannon disappeared from the neighborhood. The big kids sat at the back of the school bus and my friends and I sat at the front, so what truth there was in the legend may have changed by the time the rumor had made its way up to our seats. Here is the tale as I heard it. The weekly Dungeons and Dragons game had moved from Greg's garage to Shannon's garage. During the Friday night game, one of the major characters the guys were playing with was killed in battle. To make the death official and permanent, the player's character sheet (the piece of paper which contained all the character's stats) was tossed into a bucket and set on fire. A few minutes later, Shannon's parents came out to the garage to check up on the teens. The parents smelled the smoke and accused everyone in the garage of smoking pot. The party was immediately cancelled, and Monday morning Shannon was yanked out of school and shipped off to a drug rehab program.

And while this may sound heartless, while everyone else was worried about Shannon's well being, all I could think about were those damn Wizardry characters. In one of my earliest social engineering attempts, I devised a simple plan to get that Wizardry disk. The next day after school I showed up at Shannon's house with a backpack slung over my shoulder. I explained to Shannon's parents that I had loaned Shannon some computer disks that belonged to my father (a big lie) and that I needed to get them back. His parents told me to help myself to any disks in the room, as Shannon wouldn't need them anytime soon, so I did. Moments later I was standing in a virtual stranger's bedroom shuffling through a sea of disks, searching for the one with the word "Wizardry" written on it. I grabbed a few random handfuls of disks, shoving anything that looked interesting into my backpack, but I couldn't find Wizardry anywhere! Frantically I searched through the messy piles of disks and magazines, only to come up empty handed. Disappointed, I threw the backpack over my shoulder and was halfway out the door when it clicked. I doubled back into the room and popped open Shannon's disk drive. Out popped Wizardry. I threw the disk into my backpack and walked out of the house. I always told myself that I would return the disks when Shannon returned to the neighborhood, but he never did. A few years later his parents moved away and we never saw Shannon or his family again.

On the back of Shannon's copy of Wizardry, I discovered a program called WizFix. After running the program, users were instructed to enter their character disk into the drive. From there, you could manually modify anything in the game, from your characters' inventory to their attributes, levels, hit points, and class. I always thought of

Shannon as a dirty stinkin' cheater after discovering that program. Then I went ahead and modified all my characters too. With the help of WizFix, my dad and I finally beat Wizardry.

There were many other games we played during those days. My dad's favorite game was Lode Runner, a platform game perfectly designed for our Apple's two-button joystick. One of my personal favorites was Karateka. For my birthday one year I got a gift certificate for a local computer store. Dad drove me up to the computer store in the mall, and I ended up purchasing Karateka. I took the game home and beat it in about two hours. My dad said that was ridiculous for such an expensive game, and so we went back up to the computer store and returned it (after making a copy, of course). My dad complained to the owner that the game was too short, and they let us pick out a different game instead. Can you imagine a store letting you get away with that today? Even though it was really easy to beat, Karateka was one of my favorite Apple games due to its fluid graphics. One of my favorite Karateka tricks was booting the disk upside down, which displayed the game upside down as well! Old computer programmers had a sense of humor.

The only game my father ever banned us from playing was released by Bill Gates. Microsoft's Olympic Decathlon allowed up to six people to complete against one another in ten different events. Like the popular arcade game Track and Field, gamers made their characters run faster by banging alternating keys on the keyboard. The first time my father walked in the house and saw a bunch of my friends and I smashing his $1,000+ keyboard as hard as we could, he vetoed that game from ever being played. In fact, I seem to remember that disk getting "lost" somewhere shortly afterward. Of course, at the time it's a wonder anyone even noticed a disk missing. Between my father's BBS connections and his offline contacts, we had a stream of games arriving faster than either of us could play them.

One thing I always liked about the Apple computer was all the productivity software. Programs like Newsroom and Print Shop in particular were two programs that turned your computer into a creativity powerhouse. Broderbund's Print Shop was a simple-to-use program that allowed users to create custom greeting cards, signs, and even banners. In one of my first entrepreneurial opportunities, I began selling printed out banners to my fellow grade school classmates. I charged a quarter per letter and fifty-cents for a clipart picture that could appear at either or both ends of the banner. A "Dallas Cowboys" banner surrounded by football helmets would set a kid back $4.25. The best part about the business was that it didn't cost me a thing – I was printing the banners out at home while my father was at work! Sadly, the business was forced to file for bankruptcy the first time my dad demanded to know where all the ink from his printer ribbon and printer paper had mysteriously gone.

At the beginning of seventh grade I met a kid named Joe at school who also had an Apple computer. I bragged to him about how many games we had for our computer, and Joe asked me if I would copy some for him. I said sure, and the next day Joe brought me 2 boxes of blank disks. That's roughly 40 games (20 disks, one game per side). I had really only planned on copying a couple of disks for the guy, but I really wanted to be Joe's friend so I didn't say anything. That weekend I started copying Joe's games. I can't remember exactly how long it took to copy a disk, maybe five minutes or so per side, but I can remember getting madder and madder with each disk I copied. My dad stopped by the living room to ask what I was doing, and when I told him he got a little upset. Here I was, wearing out his expensive computer disk drives copying games for some kid at school and not getting anything in return. My dad told me not to offer to do that anymore. I spent several hours that weekend copying games. My face was hot and red and I had that feeling in my stomach you get when you know you're being used and you let it happen.

I finished copying the last of the disks late Sunday night and took the two boxes of disks to Joe Monday morning.

"Great, thanks!" he said. "I have two more boxes of blanks in my locker waiting for you!" he said.

When I tried to explain to Joe about what my dad had said, Joe just said I should try and do it when my dad wasn't around. I didn't tell him that I really didn't want to do it though. Instead I took the disks and snuck around when my dad wasn't looking and copied a few more disks for Joe. After doing five or six disks I got so pissed off that I just took what I had done at that point and gave Joe back his boxes of disks, most of them still blank.

"Some friend you are," he told me as he snatched the boxes of disks from my hands. I felt the same way about him. I don't think we ever spoke to one another again, and he transferred to another school a few years later.

There was a lesson to be learned here, although it took me several more years to finally figure it out. There was absolutely no point in trading software with kids from school. Sharing my games with my friends was one thing, but actually getting stuff in return from kids at school to build my software collection never happened.

Later that same year (seventh grade) I joined my school's newspaper staff. We put out four issues a school year, one every nine weeks. Kids were allowed to write news stories or articles about any topic they desired. There wasn't a lot of hard news contained in any of the issues. In one issue the lead story was an interview with our school's janitor. Another article tackled the hard-hitting question, "Breakdancing – Here to stay?"

I, of course, wanted to write about computers. Initially I had hoped to write a column that answered people's computer questions, but when I couldn't find anybody with any computer questions I decided to write an article about computer piracy instead. My newspaper advisor thought this was an interesting idea, so she encouraged me to get people's opinions about copying computer programs. For the next few days I carried around a small notebook, asking kids in the hallways of Independence Middle School what their opinion of software piracy was. Most kids I asked didn't even know what "piracy" was, and when I explained it to them they couldn't come up with any reasons against it. I guess free games sounded good to just about everyone! I even asked my advisor for her opinion and she said that she thought it was okay to copy software. Of course she may have been biased; our newspaper was created on pirated copies of Newsroom and Print Shop clipart that I had given her! In the end I think I ended up making up the anonymous anti-piracy quotes.

This experience put a lot of things in perspective for me. Here my dad and I were spending hours upon hours each week downloading, trading, and playing computer games, and most of the kids I went to school with didn't even know that world existed. Later that year I would

HACKERS - THE BIG CONTROVERSY
BY ROBBIE O'HARA

First of all, what is a hacker? Is a pirate someone with an eyepatch
and a wooden leg? What do these terms mean in the computer world?
And, do you think that copying copyrighted software should be illegal?
I hope you can make a decent decision after reading this article.

First of all, let me make a fact clear: There ARE hackers out there.
There is no denying that part of it. The problem is, that when you
copy something, the price goes up. After the price goes up, more
people copy it. Then, the price goes higher, so even MORE people copy
it. A vicious cycle indeed!

Well, before I tell you what some people in this school think, I will
tell you my opinion. I think that there is some wrong on both sides.
Copying software is a crime, but so are today's prices! If a record
costs from three dollars to fifteen dollars, and books can be rented
for free at library, how come software costs from twenty dollars to
several hundred? And, whenever you look at the box, it shows a GREAT
picture of a handsome guy, with his beautiful girlfriend, shooting
space creatures, with his ever-so-powerful space handgun.
Immediately, you load up the game and look at the graphics. They are
nothing like the picture on the box. Then, you pull out the
instructions, to make sure you bought the right game. Sure enough,
you did, and the instructions go something like this: "You are the
blue box. Avoid all green dots, and especially the killer red
triangle!" See my point? Well, here are some people's opinions.

---Pros---

I think that it should be legalized, so you can get a large library of
games.

It's fine for your everyday copier, but I think it's wrong for the big
time pirates.

There's nothing wrong with getting more games, is there?

Game prices are WAY too high! Copying games is the only way people
can get alot of programs.

---Cons---

Piracy is bad and shouldn't be tolerated.

Pirates should be hung for the things that they do.

I don't think that they (pirates) should be given the death penalty,
but, it should at least be more strictly enforced.

Well, no matter what people think, if piracy continues, it may
dry up the source of new and better software.

Hackers – The Big Controversy (IMS Times, 1985)

start to find friends who understood "the scene" and were in to
computers as much as I was, but at that time I felt pretty isolated.

The biggest thorn in every Apple computer owner's side was the
Commodore 64. Even in Apple magazines, advertisements for Apple
games would use screenshots from the Commodore 64 versions because
they looked so much better. There was no denying that of all the
computers available in the early 80's, the Commodore 64 had the best

sound and graphics. And because of that, Apple and IBM owners discounted the machine as a "game-playing toy" with "no practical business use." And every 12-year-old kid who wanted one agreed with them whole-heartedly! A game-playing toy with no practical business use sounded like a lot of fun to me, especially knowing that a library of free software was out there waiting for me if I was able to play the game right.

Dad and I were beginning to outgrow the Apple II, but we disagreed on what to buy next. All I really cared about was games, while dad was becoming more interested in the business side of computers, like productivity and programming. (Don't kid yourself – the guy still flies a mean plane in Flight Simulator!) Within a year, each of us would have new computers – his, a new IBM clone, and mine a Commodore 64.

When I began calling BBSes I used to use the alias "Robbie Franklin". Back then my friends and family called me "Robbie", and "Franklin" was a lame attempt to inform people that I owned a Franklin Ace 1000 computer. Unfortunately most people simply thought it was my real name. I considered changing my alias to "David Lightman" after the protagonist from the 1983 film *Wargames*, but I was afraid most people wouldn't get the reference. In 1984 however, a film came along that changed my life.

1984's *Cloak and Dagger* told the story of 11-year-old Davey Osbourne (Henry Thomas, Elliot from *E.T.*) and his imaginary spy sidekick Jack Flack (Dabney Coleman). In the film, Osbourne ends up with the titular Atari 5200 cartridge, on which secret government plans have been stored. On the run from real killers, the imaginary Flack rescues Osbourne time and time again. "Jack Flack always escapes," Osbourne tells his friend Kim during one scene. The idea of a guy who was always showing up just in the nick of time to save people really appealed to me. In the end of the movie Jack Flack doesn't come to Osbourne's rescue and he is forced to fend for himself, a kid up against the world. I liked that concept, too.

Armed with the knowledge my father had taught me in the land of Apples, I was ready to step out on my own in the Commodore world. I knew I wasn't going to have my father helping me, but I understood the game well enough to know I could pull it off. I was ready.

Jack Flack had arrived.

Chapter Four

The Adventure Begins

In the late 1970s there weren't many choices when it came to purchasing a home computer. Basically, your only choice was whether or not to purchase a TRS-80. In the early 1980s however, multiple companies began building and selling computers, each with their own reputation and personality. Apple flooded classrooms across America with new machines, and so their computers became associated with education. If you wanted to own the same kind of computer your kid most likely was using in school, you bought an Apple II. IBM computers on the other hand were marketed toward to business class working men who wanted to own the same type of computer at home that they used in the office. The Commodore 64 (C64), with its superior audio and video capabilities and lower selling price, was marketed as an inexpensive game-playing machine. That's not to say that you couldn't play games on a PC or do word processing on a C64, but there was no doubt as to which computer was best suited for a particular task.

The Commodore 64's graphics were leaps and bounds above the competition. Commodore's ability to use sprites along with its superior colors and graphic resolution blew away the competition, hands down. The C64's audio capabilities were also much more advanced than Apple's or IBM's at the time. I remember one program I had called "Led Zeppelin." It wasn't really a program per se; it was an eight-second long audio sample taken from a Led Zeppelin song that took up about a third of a floppy disk. The quality probably wouldn't seem very impressive to the MP3 generation, but compared to all the other computers that were still relying on beep-boop-boop-bops for sound effects back then it was awesome. I can't tell you how many times I played that sound clip for various people over the years just to watch their jaw drop. It worked every time.

The two people that really turned me on to Commodore computers were my friends Andy and Charon. Both of them were friends of mine who I met in person first as opposed to online, and both of them were instrumental in getting me hooked on the Commodore 64.

Andy and I first met at the age of five. Andy's family moved into our neighborhood, the two of us met, and we've been friends ever since. In fact, our entire families became friends. Our moms bowled on the same league, our dads talked cars and computers, and our sisters played together. Andy's younger brother Matt was the only odd kid out, bouncing between being forced to play house with our sisters and being routinely punched in the eye by Andy and me.

Andy's family owned the first Commodore 64 computer I ever personally laid hands on. Andy's dad had maybe twenty disks worth of games that Andy and I would play at every possible opportunity. We played Donkey Kong, which looked just about as close to the original as we could ever want, and Below the Root, a strange adventure game that involved jumping around trees, "pensing" people's thoughts and avoiding kidnappers.

Our favorite game during that time was Impossible Mission by Epyx. In the game, players must find pieces of a puzzle while avoiding getting zapped by evil robots before time runs out. The game flaunts everything that makes the C64 great. The graphics were stunning; the animation of the hero running and doing flips were as fluid as I had ever seen. While the mix of both cerebral puzzle solving combined with the action of a platformer made the game an instant classic, the main thing many people remember about the game is its audio samples. "Another visitor! Stay a while … staaaaaay forever!" It was the first time I had ever heard a game "talk," and it was mind blowing.

I cannot stress enough how advanced the Commodore 64's graphics were at the time compared to anything else that played games. The machine's processing power stood second only to real arcade machines. The idea of porting arcade games to home computers and videogame consoles was nothing new by 1984. In fact, it was becoming uncommon for popular arcade games *not* to be ported to home videogame consoles or computers. But due to limited processing power, most home versions didn't closely resemble their quarter-munching counterparts – that is, until the Commodore 64 appeared on the scene. To our young untrained eyes, the Commodore 64 version of Donkey Kong looked exactly like the arcade game we were familiar with. Equally impressive was the fact that the Commodore version *sounded* like the arcade game. Prior to that point in time home versions of arcade games always required a certain suspension of belief. Let's face it, even as ten-year-old kids we knew that the Atari 2600 version of Pac-Man didn't *really* look like the arcade version. While that didn't make it any less fun to us to play, let's just say in a side-by-side comparison no one could possibly confuse the two versions. Heck, prior to the C64 most home computers came standard with monochrome monitors and internal speakers! While Apple II arcade ports were fun, they weren't accurate. Even if the Commodore 64 versions weren't perfect, at least they were close!

I met Charon the first week of seventh grade in music class. We were attracted to each other's heavy metal t-shirts and a common aversion to the class song of the week, "You Can Sing A Rainbow." We hit it off and within a couple of months we were hanging out regularly at the local skating rink together, playing foosball and arcade games while everyone else skated safely in the normal, skating direction.

Charon also had a Commodore 64 computer that sat in his room on a homemade desk his father had built. Charon had a lot less software than Andy had, but the stuff he had was good. Charon's copies of Kung-Fu Master, Mario Bros. and Ghostbusters were some of the first games I used to trade for other games. I didn't know how into computers Charon really was, but he was into games and that was good enough for me.

During the fall of 1987 my uncle's Commodore 64 died. He told my parents that if we wanted to pay to have it fixed, we could have it. And so, as a late birthday present, I got my very own Commodore 64 along with a Datasette, Commodore's cassette tape drive. I must've whined incessantly about how ungodly slow the tape drive was because I really cannot remember using it for more than a couple of days. As an early Christmas present my parents bought me a Commodore 1541 Disk Drive to go with my computer. Things were beginning to roll.

For the first few months, I did what I had learned from my father. I copied a few games from Andy and then took those disks over to Charon's house where I would use them to trade for some more of Charon's games. Then I would take those newly acquired games back over to Andy's to trade for more games. The funny thing is, both of them would have let me copy all their software at any given time, and eventually that's what happened.

Unfortunately, neither of them seemed interested in obtaining any new software except what I was giving them! They were grateful for the games I was providing, but neither one of them spent any time trying to find other software sources. My father had spoiled me in that respect. I was used to copying, trading, uploading and downloading games all the time. When I would show up and neither of them had any new games for me to play or copy, I got frustrated.

And so, using the skills I had learned from my father, I began playing "the game" all over again. The first step was to make sure I had copies of every single program the two of them had, and so I snaked my way through their entire software collections, making copies of everything (good *or* bad) I didn't already have. For thanks in return I told the two of them that for as long as we all owned Commodore computers, they would never have to worry about obtaining software ever again; I'd take care of them. It was a bargain I would uphold for the next decade.

Before I owned a modem, one of the main ways I obtained new programs was by trading with schoolmates. This was a slow and tedious process that seldom awarded more software than headaches. The kids at school were amateurs. Here I was, a teenage computer user who had been trading software for five or six years, trying to deal with idiots and amateurs who didn't organize or label their software and had very little I wanted or needed. Still, something was better than nothing, so I routinely set up trades with classmates where I would spend an afternoon copying games for other kids in hopes of getting one or two measly programs in return.

I remember one time I set up a deal to trade a few games with another kid after school. I had crammed all my floppy disks into a small duffel bag and kept them in my locker during the school day. After the final bell rang, he and I walked together over to his house. When we arrived I found the kid's computer system was set up in his parent's living room. We had just begun to unpack all my disks when we heard someone unlocking the front door.

"Quick, hide your disks – it's my dad!" the guy yelled.

Hide my disks? It turns out the kid's dad was a preacher, who both understood and highly frowned upon computer piracy. Frantically the two of us shoved disks back into my bag, paper disk sleeves flying everywhere. Somehow we managed to hide all the disks before his father walked into the living room. Suspecting we were up to something, my friend's father sat down in the living room and watched television there for the next two hours until my parents picked me up at a previously scheduled time.

One of my favorite things to do was pick up computer magazines at the time and use them like a virtual shopping list for programs I wanted to download. I would do this at computer stores, too. I'd browse the software aisles, looking at each box to help me decide which game I was going to download later that night.

I remember on one visit to Toys-R-Us, I split off from my family and went over to the computer aisle. At the end of the aisle, under glass, was a Commodore 64. It was hooked up to a printer and monitor, also under glass. The only part that stuck out through the top of the glass was the machine's keyboards. Using the simplest program ever written, I quickly typed in "10 PRINT "Jack Flack Rules!" and "20 GOTO 10", and pressed enter. What this program should have done was fill the screen over and over with the words "Jack Flack Rules!" but the minute I pressed Enter I knew something was wrong. Instead of filling the screen with my juvenile message, the printer began printing. "Jack Flack Rules! Jack Flack Rules! Jack Flack Rules!" Someone had redirected the machine's output to the printer before I had walked up to the kiosk! Even worse, the machine's RUN/STOP key had been disabled. There was literally no way for me to stop the program from running.

After panicking for a minute, I simply walked away. I found my parents over looking at bicycles or something, so I just stood by them and tried to play cool. Hopefully, no one had seen me pulling my trick.

My parents and I walked around the store for a bit. After a while, my dad suggested that we go look at software. I told him I'd already been over there, but he insisted that I go, so the two of us walked over to the computer section. When I saw the Commodore I freaked out. The entire glass case was now filled with paper. BZZZZ, BZZZZ. The printer kept printing. "Jack Flack Rules! Jack Flack Rules! Jack Flack Rules!" You could no longer even see the computer – seemingly miles of paper were now rolled up inside the display case. Soon, a couple of employees noticed what was going on. They walked over to the display case, but neither of them had a key! At one point I remember them picking up the phone and paging the manager on duty to come to the computer area.

I don't know if dad ever saw or figured out what had happened. If so, he pretended not to. Knowing him, he would have thought it was pretty funny anyway.

By the mid 1980s the computer market was booming, and my parents decided to capitalize on this wave of interest by opening their own computer store. Yukon Software was a quaint little computer shop located a block off of Main Street in Yukon, Oklahoma. My parents signed a one-year lease for the store in the spring of 1986, and with that act Yukon Software was born. My mom would run the store during the day, while my dad would help out on his days off and weekends.

Down the left hand side of the store stood three large wooden shelves my dad built and stained by hand shortly before the store opened. Each shelf was dedicated to either IBM, Apple, or Commodore software. The front of the store had things like floppy disks, shareware packages, and mouse pads. In the middle of the store was a room with large openings allowing customers to see in. Inside the room sat a large custom computer desk (another one of my dad's woodworking creations) with three computer systems on it: an IBM XT, our trusty old Franklin Ace 1000, and a Commodore SX-64 (the portable version of the Commodore 64). The three computers ran constantly, playing games and showing off demos. My dad encouraged me to spend as much time in the room as possible so customers could see me playing the latest games and having a good time. It was labor I didn't mind one bit.

For a computer loving kid like myself, this was a dream come true. Every day after school the school bus would drop me off in front of the store, where I spent most of my afternoons and weekends. I spent a lot of my time in that center area of the store playing computer games. In the back part of the store there were a couple of smaller rooms including a tiny kitchen area and a small break room with a television. I kept my bicycle at the store so that if things got boring I could pedal around town. Located just a few stores down from us was Big Ed's Hamburgers, a burger joint with a few arcade games and pinball tables that I dropped my share of quarters into over the summer. Our store was also located directly next to a mom and pop video rental store, where we rented movies on a regular basis.

Every other week or so, huge boxes filled with the latest software would arrive. When they did I would get to help my parents sort through the piles of new games and place them on the shelves. Occasionally, my dad would do something else with them. If a really hot new game came in, dad would just open it up for us to play (and make copies of), and then take it down to his other job where he had access to a shrink-wrapping machine. After resealing the game, it was placed back on the shelves and sold as new. I don't remember this happening on a regular basis, but I do remember it happening more than once. It seemed like little more than mischievous fun at the time.

I had my own source of new Commodore games at the time: Charon's parents. Charon's parents constantly bought him the latest games, so we worked out a pretty good system where they would buy them from my parents' store. Then Charon and I would copy them and trade them with people for other new games. It was a beautiful system that worked well for everybody involved.

According to my parents, Yukon Software lost money every single month the doors were open. When the store opened, I remember someone asking us, "why would you need a *whole store* dedicated to selling computer software?" When Yukon Software opened it was the only place in town to buy blank floppy disks or computer games; six months later you could buy those things at Wal-Mart for a fraction of the price. Near the end I can remember my dad saying that Wal-Mart and Target were selling programs cheaper than he could buy them wholesale. Around that time, blank floppy disks sold for around a buck each. By ordering in bulk, my dad could get them for 80 cents each, making a $2 profit from every pack of 10 sold. Then Wal-Mart began selling disks for $5 per box. How can you compete with that? For a while my parents began buying their disks at Wal-Mart and then marking them up for resale, but everyone knows that's not a terrific business model. And it wasn't just blank disks; it was everything. I can remember my dad complaining that he was paying $28 for games with a suggested retail price of $30, and the major chains had them for $25. It was a losing battle, one shared by millions of small business owners across the globe.

A few months shy of the store's one-year anniversary, Yukon Software closed its doors for good. The hand-painted sign that hung above the store was taken down and cut up, the wooden shelves and oversized computer desk were moved into my bedroom for many years to come, and the software was sold at computer trade shows and garage sales for a fraction of what my parents paid for it. The movie rental store next to Yukon Software bought out the remainder of my parents' lease and converted the space into an indoor mini-putt course.

I was sad to see Yukon Software go, not because I was going to be losing a software connection but simply because it was cool to be able to hang out in a computer store all day long. Through the store we met tons of cool people. I really enjoyed talking to other computer owners on a regular basis about playing games, or programming, or whatever. The closure of Yukon Software definitely left a void in my hobby.

And then I got my own modem, which filled not only that void but also every free minute in my life for the next several years.

Yukon Software (1986)

Mom behind the front counter (1986)

Mom in front of software (1986)

The demo area of Yukon Software. Our IBM, Franklin Ace 1000 and Commodore SX-64 lived in here for almost a year. (1986)

Chapter Five

Bulletin Boards

The biggest limiting factor in me obtaining new software at that time was simply being a kid. Going to strangers' houses to trade software in person required begging my parents for rides to and from those houses (which they provided many, many times). My mom had a pretty good eye at spotting bad apples, and would often hang around checking people out before dropping me off at a complete lunatic's house. Often other traders wouldn't take me seriously because of my age, and trading games with classmates was more about charity than it was about getting anything good. But the modem quickly became my equalizer. Once you had a modem it didn't matter how old you were or where you lived – all that mattered was what games you had, and by the time I got my first modem, I had a lot of games.

Even before I got my own modem, my life was beginning to revolve around games. To play new games you had to get new games, and to get new games you had to have new games to trade with. Whenever possible, I would play games. Whenever I tired of playing games, I would focus on getting new games I wanted to play, and if I couldn't find any of those, I would simply copy anything I could get my hands on that I didn't have, to use later as trade bait. This endless cycle began consuming the majority of my free time.

By this point in time, the division between 300-baud and 1200-baud users had begun to widen. As the numbers suggest, 1200-baud was four times faster. At 300-baud, text moved so slowly that you could actually read words faster then you could receive them. Imagine reading a web page faster than it could load! The going rate for a 300-baud modem was around $50 at that time, while 1200-baud modems ran as high as $200. For those simply wanting to read and post messages 300-baud would suffice, but for anyone wanting to upload and download software in any bearable amount of time, 1200-baud was a necessity. Some bulletin boards even banned 300-baud callers from transferring files, limiting them to message base access only.

My first modem was only 300-baud, but that didn't stop me from uploading and downloading software all day, every day. I often woke early in the morning to start a game downloading so that it would be ready for me to play when I got home from school that afternoon. Later when I got my motorcycle drivers license, I would zip home at lunch to swap in another blank disk and begin a new download, so that after school I would have two full disks of games. I would upload and download files throughout the evening, and when my mom would issue her final "lights out" I would start one final download and then turn off the monitor so it would appear the computer had been powered down. Later I used small bits of black electrical tape to cover up any glowing LEDs that would give away my nocturnal activities. It did not take much pressure from me on my parents to convince them that my modem habits deserved their own phone line. Shortly after I began modeming my sister and I got our own phone line to share, which meant I got to use it all night, all day, and we split the evenings. It was my family's third phone line; in addition to our normal home phone number, my dad already owned a second line that he was using for his own modem use.

BBS file areas came in three basic flavors. There were those that did not condone piracy and did not allow people to upload, download or even discuss the trading of copyrighted software. I can't tell you much about those boards because when I found ones like that I quickly deleted the phone number from my dialing directory, never to call back. Then there were BBSes that had both public and private areas. On the surface they might look like a legitimate bulletin board, but word would often get out that such boards had a "back room" area that people who played their cards right could get access to. Getting pirate access on those boards required quite a bit of dancing around the topic before ever getting around to the point. Then of course there were all-out, blatantly run warez BBSes. With names like Pirate's Cove, Back Alley Access and Gamez Galore, there was no mistaking these dens of pirated software for anything other than what they were. For the most part those were the boards I called.

As I previously mentioned, there were two ways to get software – by trading in person, or by trading over phone lines. For me, it was a simple matter of logistics; there was a lot more effort involved in getting my parents to drive me all over town to other people's houses for a couple of hours to trade illegal software. Swapping files online, albeit slower, was much more convenient. Using those same techniques I had learned from my father, I found it pretty easy to boost the size of my software collection in a hurry. The key was finding two BBSes that had few common callers. Then it became a simple matter of downloading a game from one board and sending it to the other. With the credits earned from that upload, I would download a different game and send it back to the first BBS. I would continue to do this until I had all the files from both boards. Occasionally when uploading a new game to a board I would change the file name slightly and then wait and see how long that particular file took to get to all the other boards in town. The places it made it to quickly obviously shared common callers, while boards that it took a long time to get to might not have had as many. That information became valuable whenever I would find a brand new game that I hadn't seen anywhere; I would make sure to upload it as quickly as possible to all the boards that I knew shared common callers. That way I got all the credits for spreading the file – credits that could be used to download more games.

It didn't take long to earn a reputation as a good user and file trader. One of my earliest supporters was the "The Boss", sysop of The Boss BBS. The Boss BBS had three floppy drives connected to it, which was impressive considering floppy drives cost $200 apiece then. His main BBS files ran off the first drive; the second drive contained downloads, and the third always housed a blank disk for people to upload games to. So I did. Any time I got something new I'd send it to the Boss. I made it a point of filling that blank disk every time it had space available on it. Apparently this impressed the guy. One day I got a private message from The Boss, asking me to be his co-sysop and be in charge of his file areas. I accepted the position.

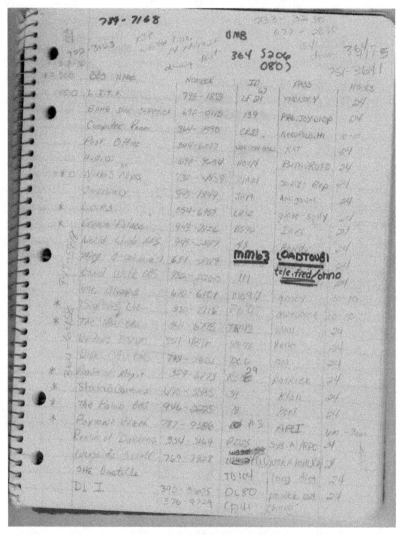

A typical page from my BBS notebooks (Date Unknown)

The first thing the Boss begged me to do was buy a faster modem. I knew he was right and I desperately wanted a 1200-baud modem. The problem was, I had no real source of income and there was no way I could come up with the $200 needed for a faster modem. The Boss told me he would come up with something. A few weeks later, the Boss told me he had something for me: a brand new 1200-baud modem still new in the box that he was selling for only $75. Somehow I talked my parents into buying it for me. Maybe my dad felt sorry for me putting along at 300-baud – he had upgraded to 1200-baud long ago on his PC.

My getting a 1200-baud modem at that moment in time was kind of like buying a hot rod for a teenager who already had a dozen speeding tickets. With a modem four times as fast, I could do four times as much trading. I didn't spend any less time online – the games simply began flowing in and out that much faster. While files were downloading from one board I would already be planning on where I would be sending them next. Instead of saving time, getting a faster modem just made me that much more addicted.

While 1200-baud was okay for transferring a game or two, any mass amount of trading was painfully slow via phone lines regardless of modem speeds. When you found a good source of software that you could trust, it would be to your benefit to set up a trade "in person." Just like the Apple days, there were always trade negotiations. For a long time I had less software than most other people, which mean a lot of the time I (and by "I" I mean "my parents") had to do the driving. There were always two rounds of negotiations on these deals. The first round involved negotiation with the other party, while the second round involved negotiation with my parents for a ride. Truth be told, both of my parents were great sports, considering how many times I begged them for rides to these people's houses twenty or thirty miles away for the sole purpose of getting more games.

Most of these trades consisted of the same routine. First, I would pack all of my software (and maybe a spare disk drive) into my parent's car, and get taxied over to the person's house. While I was busy unloading my things, my parents would quickly survey the person's home. These trades were set up online between people who might not even know each other's real names, much less where they lived, what kind of person they were or even how old they were. That was always a fun surprise; adults assumed that another adult would be coming over, while kids always assumed they would be meeting another kid. More than once my parents dropped me off on the front porch of a surprised adult who was expecting someone twenty or thirty years older than myself to show up. By the time I was a teenager I had spent more time behind computer keyboards than most adults had. As a result, I had developed the typing skills of an adult. I could easily type 70-80 words per minute by then. One guy who came to our house thought I was pulling his leg and kept asking to see my father.

By trading software with people in person, I met a lot of interesting characters. The first time I went to Dr. Phrackenstein's house, he had moved his computer desk into his walk in closet. There sat the two of us, copying software while sitting in some guy's closet. Another guy insisted on blessing each disk and would pray that a copied game would work. That was weird. One guy (who was ten or fifteen years older than I was) had a bunch of his friends over drinking beer while he and I traded games. While copying software, one of them said he had something to show us in the kitchen. On the stove the guy had placed a fork on top of one of the burners. He then showed us how he could make a fork dance by shocking the burner with his stun gun. That was one of the few times I was ever really concerned for my safety. I didn't tell my parents about the incident at the time. If I had, there's no way they would have kept dropping me off at strange people's homes.

But, more often than not, trades were usually uneventful. I would dig through another person's software collection while they thumbed through mine. Then we would take turns copying each other's software, making small talk as the computer's drives spun and lights flashed. Remember, this was still pre-multitasking – you couldn't play games on your computer while you were copying them. A big part of trading software in person involved coming up with creative ways to fill the awkward silence.

Trading software in person and trading software online fed each other. The minute I arrived home from trading games with someone I would immediately start calling bulletin boards to upload the new programs I had just acquired. And of course, I was still downloading every game I could find online. The problem with software was, a program was only valuable when you were the only one who had it. Once you had given a copy out, the value dropped rapidly. I can remember many occasions where after trading a game to someone, I would turn around and try and trade that game to as many people as possible as quickly as possible before the other person had a chance to. By then I was calling maybe a hundred different bulletin boards on a regular basis, so every time I got a new program I would begin systematically dialing down the list, sending it to every board that didn't already have it.

And true to my word, I offered every new program I got to Charon and Andy for getting my collection started. I also made sure to upload every new program I got my hands on to The Boss. The Boss' BBS was known as a hot spot for new software thanks to me. I kept it well stocked.

The problem with a bunch of kids trading software with one another is that they eventually run out of new sources. Without new places to get software, the same people end up sending the same software around the same circles over and over again. One solution to this was calling long distance bulletin boards. Computer users in different area codes had different pools of software, which meant most likely you had software they didn't have, and vice versa. Calling long distance was a great way to build up your software library with unique titles if you could afford it. Unfortunately, we couldn't.

That didn't stop my friend Charon and I from devising a plan. Every summer, my family took a road trip to Chicago to visit my dad's relatives. Before our trip in 1987, Charon and I spent the two weeks prior to my family's vacation calling bulletin boards in the Chicago area, registering accounts. Back then, sysops treated callers from other area codes with great respect since those callers were spending their own money to call long distance. Having long distance users call your BBS was considered very prestigious. Suspicious bulletin board owners would often call and verify that long distance callers were indeed who they said they were. We assumed that would occur, and as expected several of the Chicago BBS owners called us at our homes in Oklahoma and verified that we were truly out-of-state callers. The key was to spend as little time online as possible. Once our accounts were verified and set up, we waited until we got to Chicago to launch the second half of our plan.

In the back of my parents' van, packed next to our suitcases full of clothes sat my Commodore 64. Once we arrived at my grandma's house, Charon and I set up shop in granny's spare bedroom. The two of us then spent every spare moment of that weeklong vacation calling those Chicago boards and downloading games, without the long distance charges! In all we downloaded dozens of new programs that no one in Oklahoma had ever seen before. Our plan had worked perfectly!

Sometimes, when people would run out of new programs to trade with, they would make new ones. "Making them" very rarely meant "programming them from scratch." Sometimes it meant simply changing the name of a program to look like a new one, or altering the text within a game to make it seem like a new game. I remember downloading "Archon III" only to become disappointed later when I discovered it was really just Archon II with a new (fake) title screen.

One program I "made" was a voice digitizer. The program itself came from one of the computer magazines of the time that included programs you could yourself type into the computer. This particular program allowed you to digitize your voice using a Datasette, Commodore's cheap cassette tape player. The first step was to type the entire program into the computer, which I did. Once I was finished with that, I then created a recording of my voice. This was done on my portable stereo. I think the program allowed you to record about 20 seconds of audio, so I made a short recording stating my name and announcing to the world how cool I was. The final step was using the program and the Datasette to get my voice recording into the computer. After a couple of days of trial and error, I finally got the program to work.

The end results were, well, not that impressive. I mean, it was extremely cool to hear my own voice coming from a computer's speaker for the first time, but the quality wasn't that great. My voice sounded like it was being broadcast over an AM radio that was slightly out of tune and in the next room. Still, I was excited to have something that no one else had, and I quickly uploaded the file to several local bulletin boards. One of those boards was Ball of Confusion, run by a guy named Arcane (who I would later become friends with). After uploading the file to Arcane's board, I send him a message, asking him what he thought of the file.

After listening to it, his first question back to me was, "Who was that?"

"It's me!" I replied to him.

"Oh. What did it say?" he asked.

By this point I was losing enthusiasm. I repeated the message back to him.

"Oh. It sounded like you were on the moon," was his final comment back to me.

As quickly as it had began, my Commodore recording career was over.

The hottest game to come out in 1987 was California Games by Epyx. I knew two different people who had purchased the game, but it had such wicked copy protection that it was nearly impossible to copy. Whoever was able to bring California Games to Oklahoma was going to be *the* man. I decided that person was going to be me.

By now I had a job working nights and weekends at a small concession stand with Andy and Charon, and was bringing home decent money for a young teenager. Several of the games I had downloaded recently contained the number for "The Purple Dragon", a BBS out in California. I knew if anyone had California Games, The Purple Dragon would. I asked my parents for permission to call long distance and download the game. They said it was fine, as long as I agreed to pay for any long distance charges that appeared on the phone bill. We agreed, and I set off to find the Purple Dragon.

That night I set up an account on the board and was validated. I was right, the board did have California Games online, but unfortunately I didn't have enough credits to download it. Credits could only be obtained by uploading something the sysop didn't already have. I ended up uploading several of the games I had just got from my Chicago adventures, all of which were pretty new. It burned me up that I was paying long distance phone charges to upload games to someone else, but there was no other option. I had to have *that* game!

Once I had enough credits I began downloading California Games. In stores the game fit on two sides of a disk, but I guess the extra information included by the cracking group expanded the release to three disks. I watched the clock, figuring my phone bill charges minute by minute. Halfway through the second disk I figured I had already spent more than it would have taken to just buy the stupid thing, but I didn't care. If I bought it, I wouldn't be able to copy it. At that point it was more about the game's trading power than the actual game itself.

In the end I want to say it cost me around $50 to download a game that I could have purchased in any computer store in town for $30. But that wasn't the point. I began uploading California Games all over town, and I became somewhat of a local hero. Even private BBSes that I did not have access to previously began sending me private invitations asking me to join their ranks. The fifty bucks was money well spent.

One of the new boards that became available to me was a BBS called The Wizard's Scroll, run by a guy named The Trooper. The Trooper was almost ten years older than me and was a complete dick, not just to me but also to everyone who knew him. In retrospect, he treated me like I treated those other kids at school with crappy software collections. To him most local users were slime, not even worthy of groveling at his feet. And to him, somehow I personified everything that was lame about local users. The guy had posts on his BBS talking about what a punk kid I was, and when people would come to my defense he would delete their responses.

The Trooper's co-sysop was a troll named Archangel. There's no denying that between the two of them The Wizard's Scroll had some of the best software on any local BBS – not that we locals ever got to download anything. The Trooper was known for giving local users enough access to see all the new games he had, but not enough access to download anything.

This began to change when word got out that I had obtained a copy of California Games. At first, The Trooper began telling people that I was lying about having the game. I put a stop to that by uploading the first of the game's three disks to his BBS, and holding the other two for ransom.

I got a message through Dr. Phrackenstein (a mutual friend of ours) that The Trooper and Archangel wanted to trade games with me. The deal would be on my own turf; they could come to my house and trade with me there. In return for California Games, the two of them promised me access to The Wizard's Scroll along with all the latest games, which they would bring with them. A date and time were set.

That weekend, The Trooper and Archangel along with Dr. Phrackenstein all arrived at my parent's house. Keep in mind that I was still 13 or 14 years old at the time, and these guys were in their early to mid 20s. The very first thing they wanted to do was see California Games. I showed it to them, and they made a copy. While The Trooper and Dr. Phrackenstein kept me busy, Archangel went through my complete disk box, pulling out every single new game and making copies of them. After a few minutes I began getting nervous. I asked to see the stuff they brought and they said it was out in their car. They said when they were done copying my stuff they would go get their disks. When they were done copying every new game I had, I watched the three of them walked out to the car, get in, and drive away, laughing the entire time. I had just given up everything I had in trade for nothing. Dr. Phrackenstein later told me that he had been set up too and had no prior knowledge of their plans to rip me off.

Even though I was one of the best traders in the area, I was still just a little kid. I can remember sitting in my room crying that night. For the first time in a long time, I turned my computer off.

Fortunately, most of the other people I met and traded with weren't jerks like The Trooper and Archangel. After a while, the biggest problem I had wasn't with personalities; it was with finding people who had programs I didn't already have! My small collection of thirty floppy disks had grown to over three hundred in a very short amount of time. It became very time consuming to trade with one person at a time.

Through a friend of a friend, I heard about a Commodore computer club called Univision. Univision meetings were held once a month, and members of the club were encouraged to bring their computers and set them up. From what I had heard, the club turned a blind eye to any illegal software trading that was going on at their club. If trading with one person at a time was good, then trading with 20 or 30 at a time sounded even better.

Chapter Six

Copyfests

Univision was an Oklahoma City Commodore 64 user's group and the brainchild of Stephen Love, author of His Majesty's BBS software (HMBBS). The purpose of Univision was for C64 owners to meet, discuss computers, exchange information, and provide technical assistance to one another. At least, that's how the club was publicly advertised. In reality, meeting attendees traded a lot more software than they did technical solutions. I don't ever recall seeing even as much as a simple presentation at any of the club's meetings.

Univision meetings took place from 9am to 5pm on the last Saturday of every month in the meeting room of a seedy downtown hotel. The neighborhood the hotel resided in was not great. The swimming pool stood empty and wallpaper drooped from the interior walls. Parents stood guard as their children carried loads of expensive computer equipment into the hotel's meeting room. I don't personally remember ever feeling as though I were in danger, but I do remember my mother explicitly telling me that I was not to leave the property under any circumstances.

It would be tough to refer as those monthly assemblies as meetings – "gatherings" is a more accurate term. "Meeting" insinuates some sort of official agenda or structure. There was none of that to be found at Univision. After paying your monthly entry fee ($5, I believe) members were free to do whatever they wanted to do. Some people showed off their latest software or programs they had written while others set up small gaming tournaments, challenging others to bracket-style game challenges. Of course, I was there for one reason: to trade software. During each meeting I would methodically work my way around the room from person to person, seeking out any programs I didn't already have. Unfortunately, among the Univision crowd that usually didn't amount to be much. Most of the members of Univision were average computer users, not game-hungry software collectors such as myself. Regardless, Univision meetings were still a lot of fun to attend. If nothing else you got to hang out with fellow Commodore 64 owners for a day, and that was okay by me.

At one of the meetings I mentioned to some of the guys "in charge" that I had an unused CP/M cartridge with me. Not only had I never used the thing, I didn't even know what one would be used for. The entire time I owned a Commodore computer I never once saw a use for the thing, but for some reason Stephen Love wanted it. The older guys checked it out and asked me how much I wanted for it. I had no idea of the cart's value, so I asked them what it was worth. Love told me he'd make me a deal; he'd trade me a year's membership in Univision for the cartridge. That sounded good to me, so shortly before lunch I gave Love the cartridge, and headed downstairs to grab some lunch.

When I started down the stairs I remembered that I had left my money back in the room, so I turned around and went back. When I got just outside the doorway I could hear all the adults laughing about the transaction. Some of them were saying how stupid I was to give them that cartridge for nothing. I can still remember Stephen Love himself referring to me as "that dumb kid."

I wasn't a dumb kid. I was Jack Flack.

A few minutes later, those same three or four adults went downstairs to grab a bite as well. The minute they did, I walked right over to their computers. Stephen Love always brought his disk box from home, but never traded software with people. That would be unethical! So, I decided to help Mr. Love share the wealth. I began going through his personal disk box, picking out anything that looked good and copying it. I didn't know how much time I was going to have, so I worked quickly. In the back of his disk box, I struck gold. The next to last two disks in his container were the blank master disks for HMBBS. These were the unedited master copies that people received when they purchased his expensive bulletin board software. Those were the first two things I copied. The last two disks in his box were his actual BBS disks – the real live disks he ran his BBS from. I copied those, too. Those disks contained every single one of his users' real names, phone numbers, and passwords. I copied the disks as quickly as possible, labeled them "secret one" through "secret four" and shoved them somewhere in the middle of my disk box. Nobody laughs at Jack Flack.

I stewed the whole way home. For a while I had tried convincing several friends of mine to join Univision so we could all trade software in one central location, but after that incident I decided I didn't want to put any more money into Univision's pockets. Besides, Univision members weren't really my crowd anyway. What I wanted was to hold my own copyfest. I wanted to dispense with the pretense of a computer club. I wanted people to get together for the sole purpose of trading software. The only thing I needed was someone old enough to rent a room for me.

The first person I turned to was The Boss. Unfortunately, for some reason both his BBS and his voice phone lines had suddenly become disconnected. Not knowing what was going on I moved to another friend, The Wizard (no relation to The Wizard's Scroll). I made The Wizard a pretty good deal – all he had to do was reserve the hotel's meeting room on his credit card. My job would be to invite 20 known good traders to the party. Each person was to bring their computer and software collections and would pay $3 to attend the copyfest. It cost around $40 to rent the room. Not only would The Wizard get to pocket any profits, but he'd also get to attend and have access to the hottest software around. He agreed to the deal and rented the room.

Once the room had been reserved I went through the local bulletin board scene and created a "Who's Who" list of local modem users. Invites were sent electronically, and the following week elite members of the local BBS scene began showing up at the Grand Continental Hotel, most of them having been dropped off by their parents. Of the 20 people I invited, very few of them were old enough to drive. I'm sure The Wizard felt more like a chaperone than anything.

The Grand Continental Hotel's conference room was located in the back of the hotel and was somewhat difficult to find. Fearing that our attendees would have a difficult time finding the party, I went down to the lobby to instruct the clerk to point anyone walking in with computer equipment our way. When the girl at the front desk asked what we were doing, I told her the truth. "We're having a copyfest." Like she knew what that was.

That first copyfest took place on a Friday night, and for about four hours that night the elite of the Oklahoma City Commodore modem scene sat in the Grand Continental Hotel copying games. Box fans were brought in to cool the hot air generated by the twenty computer systems working overtime. I can't remember seeing a single computer in the room set up for playing games; no one wanted to waste their time doing so. Every computer in the room was slaving away making backups of backups, copies of copies.

And while the twenty of us sat in a cheap hotel room, copying software, breaking laws and having fun, on the other side of town federal agents had just kicked in The Boss' front door to arrest him.

That night on the evening news, I heard about the arrest of Bruce Heikes, a.k.a. The Boss of Boss BBS. According to the following morning's newspaper, The Boss had been spending his weekends dialing his local Sprint provider with his computer, trying random long distance codes. (There was no skill involved in this – there were many programs available at the time that would do this for you.) If the code didn't work, the program moved on to the next one. If it did work, it was saved in a log file for later use. Working codes could be used for free long distance calling, or they could be traded for various other goods: usually either software or access, although trading codes for hardware was not unheard of. Apparently, some codes also corresponded to credit card numbers as well, which may or may not explain where my cheap, still new in the box 1200 baud modem from The Boss had come from ...

A couple of days later I asked my parents to take me over to The Boss' house. When we got there we found it was basically empty. There was an overturned chair in the living room and a card table that we could see in the kitchen, but everything else was gone. My first thought was that he was screwed. My second thought was that I was screwed, too.

My parents realized I was upset over the whole ordeal, but I'm not sure they really knew why. My biggest fear at that point was that the feds were going to come knocking on my door next. I was The Boss' right hand man on his BBS. My real name and contact information were listed at the top of his user files. And even though I hadn't been hacking along with him, even the most cursory search of his BBS logs would show the massive amounts of software I was regularly uploading to him. For weeks I walked around school with a sinking pit in my stomach, afraid that each day when I got home from school I would find flashing lights and snipers waiting for me in the trees. Fortunately, for whatever reason, I was never contacted by any law enforcement agency about the event. I did however learn to not give my real name and phone number out quite so freely.

There were many different flavors of subculture in the computer world. Aside from piracy (which was so common that people rarely even referred to it as something illegal), many boards displayed the HPAC badge: Hacking, Phreaking, Anarchy, and Carding. Later, HPAC was changed to HPVAC to include Virus programming.

"Carding" refers to the illegal use of other people's credit cards. Technically, "carding" something means buying something using someone else's credit card without their permission, although there are other various aspects of carding. Most people I knew who dealt in credit card numbers weren't using them to buy things, but rather to pay for their long distance phone bills. As programs continued to grow in size, long

City Couple Charged As 'Hackers'

An Oklahoma City couple are computer "hackers" who used their home computer to illegally obtain information from a long-distance telephone company, prosecutors alleged Thursday.

Bruce A. Heikes, 31, and his wife, Gisela, 23, were charged in Oklahoma County District Court with a felony count of conspiring to violate the state's computer crime law and a felony count of violating the law.

The two, who work at a bakery, face up to 20 years in prison and $105,000 in fines on the two counts, a prosecutor said.

The two are accused of using their home computer and a telephone to get into U.S. Sprint's credit card computer network, then search for authorization codes — nine-digit numbers used by customers to charge long-distance calls.

U.S. Sprint reported it detected use of the personal computer Aug. 7 and was able to trace the call Monday. The computer placed 351 calls between 12:29 p.m. and 4:51 p.m. Monday, as often as once every 27 seconds, in its systematic search for codes, authorities said.

Assistant District Attorney Brad Miller said some computer hackers are known to sell illegally obtained codes. At least 100 codes were found Wednesday in a search of the Heikes' home, 8320 NW 80, he said.

distance callers found themselves online longer and longer to download the latest games. Using someone else's credit cards to pay those bills were a dirty way to circumvent that problem. Trafficking cards was also a status thing. Some BBSes required you to submit a stolen credit card number during the new user application, just to show you were serious. While I never once used a stolen credit card number, I did have a stash of working codes at my disposal should I need one. Seeing The Boss get busted was enough to steer me clear of this activity for life. In fact, none of my close friends were into carding. We certainly weren't in a position to order things using other people's credit cards – our parents would have become pretty suspicious if packages had begun arriving on our doorsteps.

What we were into, however, was phreaking and hacking.

The word "phreak" is a conglomeration of the words "phone" and "freak", and it was certainly not a new concept when we first began dabbling in it. The infamous John Draper (AKA Captain Crunch) first exploited the phone system back in the early 70's by blowing a 2600mhz tone into his phone, granting him operator-like access. Two ingenious hackers named Steve Jobs and Steve Wozniak (who would go on to form Apple Computers) took the technology behind Draper's tone generator and began mass-producing them in little blue boxes, which they sold to fellow college students. The boxes were became known as Blue Boxes, and the art of using them was known as Blue Boxing.

While the technology and knowledge previously existed, before the personal computer storm of the 1980's there was no good way to archive and share this knowledge with the general public. Information about Blue Boxes found their way to the computer underground, and from there they spread like wildfire. As phreakers continued to find different ways to exploit Ma Bell, each new invention would be shoved into a project box, named after a color, and shared with fellow phreakers everywhere. There were Black Boxes, there were Cheese Boxes, but the most useful (and probably most infamous) of all was the Red Box.

The idea behind a Red Box is quite simple. Whenever you put coins into a payphone, the payphone generates tones. A nickel generates one short beep, a dime produces two and a quarter sounds off five. A Red Box was a small device that could reproduce those tones and fool a payphone (or a live operator) into thinking real coins had been deposited into the phone, thus allowing the caller to use any payphone for free. Most Red Boxes of the time were built out of modified Radio Shack tone dialers, but we had our own way of making them. Prong, a friend of mine, disassembled one of those Hallmark greeting cards that allowed you to record a personal greeting for a loved one and crammed the guts into a small plastic box that would fit in the palm of your hand. One small switch toggled the device between record and play modes. The other button played back the sound. The "quarter" tone was then transferred to the device. To make free phone calls from a pay phone, all you had to do was hold the device up to the phone's speaker and play the tones. The payphone would register the tones as real coins, and off you went. I have heard many times from many people that this didn't work; it did, I can assure you. In fact it worked as recently as last year, when I found the small device, threw some fresh batteries in it and tried it out once again. Only once did I have any problems with my Red Box – on a weekend in Minnesota, it got so cold that the batteries began to drain and the tones began to slow down, so much that the operator broke in on my phone conversation, accused me of not depositing real coins, and promptly disconnected my call!

Red Boxes, Blue Boxes, and Beige Boxes (homemade lineman handsets) were the only boxes I personally ever saw used. Most of the other boxes I saw were so outlandish or outdated that I never even tried them. Black Boxes were supposed to allow owners to get free phone calls. The idea behind it was that the voltage of your phone line was supposedly higher when it was ringing than after you answered it, so this device in theory could boost the voltage on your line so that the phone company couldn't tell that you had ever answered your phone. Since you don't get billed if someone's phone just rings and rings, it was supposed to allow for people to be able to call you for free. I don't know if it worked; the thought of shooting electricity through my parents' phone line kind of scared me. There was a Cheese Box, which supposedly turned your home phone into a pay phone (which you could then theoretically use a Red Box and make free calls through). There were boxes that allowed you to put people on hold, to combine your phones and do your own conference calling, even boxes that would allow you to destroy people's modems. All in all there were literally hundreds of box plans available. Like I said, many of them sounded pretty fanciful and I doubt that many of them worked.

Another aspect of phreaking just involved trading phone information. For example, there was a three-digit number (which still works on some payphones!) that would cause a payphone to, for lack of a better word, "reboot". Dialing this three-digit number will cause the payphone to go dead for 3-5 minutes. You won't be able to get a dial tone and the phone will not ring. Then there was the "sweep" phone number, which was a phone number that produced a sweeping sound. The rumor was that if the sound locked at a single frequency, your line was tapped. We were never sure if it was true or not, but that didn't stop us from calling it from time to time to make sure our lines weren't "tapped."

Of all the HPVAC activities, most of our time was spent hacking. War Dialing (which got its name from technique popularized in the movie *WarGames*) was the art of making you computer dial entire phone exchanges, searching for listening modems on the other end. There were several programs available that would help you find "targets." Most of them simply asked you for a beginning phone number (555-0001) and an ending number (555-9999). Once the program had that information, it would simply begin dialing phone numbers. Anytime it found a computer modem on the other end, it would set that number aside for you in a separate log file. After hours of dialing, all one had to do was try the numbers in that log file and look for interesting things. During the 1980's no one had even dreamt of caller ID, so even if you did call and hang up on people there wasn't much they could do about it. Through war dialing, we discovered lots of interesting computer systems out there just begging to be explored. Probably one of the most interesting was one that identified itself as Pizza Hut. Through its primitive menu system callers could download weekly sales and other not-so-interesting stuff, but the thought of actually logging in to a corporate machine was pretty thrilling. We discovered lots of modems during the time frame – everything from schools to banks to businesses. We were never able to change our grades or start World War III like David Lightman did in Wargames, but we did have lots of fun poking around.

In the mid 1980's, several Commodore 64 hackers in the Oklahoma area joined together and formed H.I.T., which stood for the Hacker Information Team. The members of H.I.T. shared the information each of them was discovering during that exciting era. The first time I got access to the secretive H.I.T. message boards, I read every single post and saved them all to disk. Then I borrowed Charon's printer and printed them all out. Then Charon made his mom buy him new printer ribbon. Again, it wasn't the best system, but it worked for us.

The members of H.I.T. made some good information available to the rest of us, but unlike some of those guys, I was too afraid to try most of it. I was more afraid of what my parents would do to me than what the phone company might say.

My old friend Dr. Phrackenstein ("Phrack", for short) was a member of H.I.T. (which may have been how I got my invitation; I can't quite remember), and the two of us spent many late nights on the phone talking about phone phreaking. Phrack would often call my house while he was connected to either a conference call or a party line. I'd pick up my phone in the middle of the night only to find 50 or 60 other people all chatting up a storm.

Phrack was a pretty mischievous guy. Phrack was one of the people I knew that had three-way calling, and he would often use it to play tricks on people. One time the two of us pulled a prank on a schoolmate of mine that went south in a hurry. There was a kid in school who I had traded software with, and Phrack came up with an idea for a funny prank. I would call the guy with Phrack quietly on the line. The idea for the joke was that during the conversation, Phrack would "break in" to the call, announcing himself as a federal agent and informing us that we were both busted. It sounded pretty harmless.

We called the guy, and just as we had planned I started talking to the guy about pirated software. Suddenly Phrack pretended to break in to our conversation, telling us that the line had been tapped and that we were both going to jail. Phrack then disconnected the line and that was that – or so I thought.

Rob in front of his Commodore (1985)

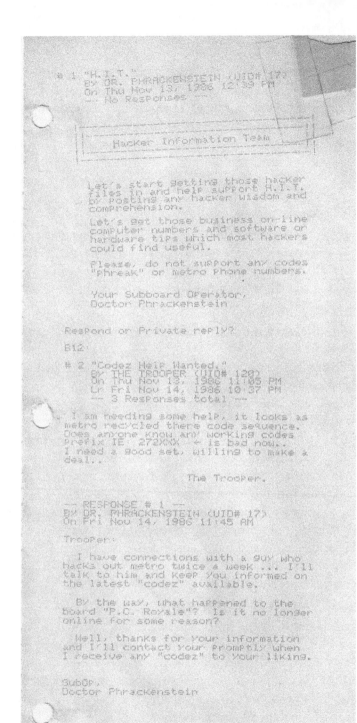

```
# 1 "H.I.T."
   BY DR. PHRACKENSTEIN (UID# 17)
   On Thu Nov 13, 1986 12:39 PM
   -- No Responses --


   +---------------------------------+
   |  Hacker Information Team        |
   +---------------------------------+


     Let's start getting those hacker
     files in and help support H.I.T.
     by posting any hacker wisdom and
     comprehension.

     Let's get those business on-line
     computer numbers and software or
     hardware tips which most hackers
     could find useful.

     Please, do not support any codes
     "phreak" or metro phone numbers.


     Your Subboard Operator,
     Doctor Phrackenstein


   Respond or Private reply?

   B12:

# 2 "Codez Help Wanted."
   BY THE TROOPER (UID# 120)
   On Thu Nov 13, 1986 11:05 PM
   Lr Fri Nov 14, 1986 10:37 PM
   -- 3 Responses total --

   I am needing some help. it looks as
   metro recycled there code sequence.
   Does anyone know any working codes
   Prefix IE: 272XXX  + is bad now..
   I need a good set. willing to make a
   deal..

                    The Trooper.


   -- RESPONSE # 1 --
   BY DR. PHRACKENSTEIN (UID# 17)
   On Fri Nov 14, 1986 11:45 AM

   Trooper:

     I have connections with a guy who
   hacks out metro twice a week ... I'll
   talk to him and keep you informed on
   the latest "codez" available.

     By the way, what happened to the
   board "P.C. Royale"?  Is it no longer
   online for some reason?

     Well, thanks for your information
   and I'll contact your promptly when
   I receive any "codez" to your liking.

   SubOp,
   Doctor Phrackenstein
```

File capture from H.I.T. (1986)

The next day at school, the kid told me that in a panic he had taken all his diskettes and thrown them in his swimming pool, underneath his pool's liner in order to hide them. Oops. I felt pretty bad about the whole thing, and when I told the kid that it was just a joke I'm pretty sure he didn't talk to me again for a few years.

Word about our first copyfest had spread, and soon we had begun planning the second. While our first copyfest had taken place on a Friday night and spanned three hours, our second one was planned for a Saturday day, giving us a solid eight hours for copying games. Our second copyfest kicked off on a cold February morning in 1987.

Mister X and Umbra Sprite, two of the guys who came to our first copyfest, brought a third guy with them to our second party – a pudgy kid named Arcane. I knew Arcane through the BBS he ran (Ball of Confusion, named after Love and Rockets' version of the Temptations song), but had never met him in person before. Mister X had driven the three of them in his dad's car to the copyfest. He was fifteen at the time (the oldest of the group, but still not old enough to legally drive). The first thing that struck me about Arcane was that he had some awesome 80's hair – I mean, we're talking some Flock of Seagulls, higher-than-it-was-long hair. Arcane and I hit it off right from the beginning. Around lunchtime, Arcane asked Umbra Sprite multiple times if he was hungry and wanted to walk with him to McDonald's to get something to eat. After being turned down multiple times by Umbra, Arcane asked me if I would walk with him instead. I agreed, and as we were walking out the door, Umbra yelled, "hey, since you guys are going to McDonald's, pick me up an order of McNuggets!"

The two of us, bundled in matching trench coats and braving the cold winter wind, walked the mile to the nearest McDonald's. Arcane and I ordered our lunch and Umbra's McNuggets at the same time. I asked Arcane if he wanted to wait until we were leaving to order Umbra's food so it would still be warm, but he just shot me a look. After eating lunch, we began the long walk back to the hotel. As we walked, Arcane opened Umbra's box of McNuggets and had begun holding them up in the air one by one, making sure each one was nice and cold before holding up the next one. There was something about this kid I liked. Of course,

Umbra didn't even notice that his McNuggets were ice cold when we got back, and the whole incident became our little secret.

Arcane and Umbra lived in Norman, Oklahoma, about 40 miles southeast of my hometown of Yukon. Due to the distance, Arcane and I worked out a deal with our parents; mine would drive me out to his place in Norman if his parents would bring me home. Occasionally we'd talk them into letting me spend the entire weekend in Norman.

Arcane had a Honda Elite scooter that harnessed a sarcastically massive 80cc's of power under its white plastic shell. According to Honda's website, top speed for the Elite was a blazing 42 miles per hour, but I doubt Arcane's poor scooter ever got anywhere near that speed, especially with both of our fat asses on it. Before I had my own motorcycle I used to take my skateboard to Norman with me so Arcane could pull me around the neighborhood on it using his scooter. Arcane's parents were much less restrictive than mine, and so even as young teenagers we would often leave the house at 2 or 3 in the morning for a late night doughnut run.

Umbra lived only a couple of miles away from Arcane, so a visit to Arcane's also usually meant the two of us would visit Umbra. Umbra always had new games, usually bought from the store. During our visits, Arcane and I would give him copies of our games and would then spend the rest of our visit trying to figure out how to copy his original disks.

One funny thing about Umbra was that his glasses were always being broken. The reason for that was that any object thrown in any room would always end up hitting Umbra in the face. I don't know why, but I witnessed it several times and knew it to be true. I must've seen Umbra's glasses break on half a dozen occasions, and I'm not sure I met him many more times than that. One time while Umbra was out of the room, Arcane explained this phenomenon to me. To prove his point, when Umbra re-entered the room Arcane threw a floppy disk at him. Like playing cards, floppy disks don't fly straight like a Frisbee; they curve, arc and swoop before striking their target. As if on cue, the disk cut high toward the ceiling, did a flip, came down, sped up and hit Umbra directly in the face, breaking his glasses. Even as Umbra was crying and throwing us out of his house, Arcane and I were laughing so hard we could barely stand.

In the state of Oklahoma you can get a motorcycle license at the age of 14. For my 14th birthday, I got my own mode of transportation, a Honda CB 125 motorcycle. Umbra owned a scooter as well, a Honda 50. Norman was too far for me to drive to on my motorcycle (one of the stipulations of being a young motorcycle driver was that you were not supposed to exceed 35mph). Instead, my dad would load my motorcycle up into the back of his pickup, and we would tote it to Norman that way. Once there, Arcane, Umbra and I cruised Norman, looking for fun, trouble, or both.

One of the funniest stories about our rides involved the time Arcane brought his scooter to my house. Norman, where Arcane lived, was a college town, the perfect location for a scooter owner. Yukon, however, wasn't suited very well for one. To get from my house into town you had to take one road with a 55mph speed limit, hop on another back road for a couple of miles, and take a third dirt road for another mile.

While waiting to turn right out of my neighborhood and onto the high-speed road, I saw a large semi truck coming over the hill, heading toward us. There wasn't enough time to pull out in front of the truck, so I waited and, with the clutch pulled in, revved my engine. Arcane heard the sound of my engine revving and thought I was going, so he opened the throttle on his scooter and took off, directly into me. I hit the brake immediately to prevent myself from flying out in front of the oncoming semi. When I turned around and looked behind me, I saw two legs sticking straight up into the air. Arcane had somehow managed to get the front of his scooter wedged underneath the rear of my motorcycle, but that wasn't the funniest part. When he came to a sudden stop, he had flipped completely over the front of his scooter. His head was down by the front tire while his legs kicked around aimlessly up in the air. It took a fair amount of prying to get the two vehicles separated. Once they were apart, we decided to visit a friend who could help us repair the two vehicles. As we hit the dirt road, we discovered that large motorcycle tires handle dirt roads much better than tiny scooter wheels. Halfway down the dirt road, Arcane's handlebars begin shaking violently just moments before his scooter wobbled off the road and dove nose first into a ditch. Arcane and his scooter were dirty, but undamaged. That was the last time Arcane brought his scooter to Yukon.

Throughout 1987 and 1988, my friends and I continued business as usual, building our software collections by trading online as much as possible, holding our own copyfests and attending ones organized by other people. Other people's copyfests rarely seemed to be as good as ours were. One particularly craptastic copyfest was thrown by a moron named Beach Boy, sysop of Daytona Beach BBS. Beach Boy's father owned a small TV repair shop and the copyfest I attended took place in the back of the store among piles of old, broken television tubes. During the copyfest, one of Beach Boy's friends began asking me if I had a copy of Winter Games. I had it, but didn't have the means to copy it – it took a special program to do. The guy shrugged and went on.

When I got home from the copyfest, I had a message on my answering machine from Arcane. When I returned his call, he asked me if I had a copy of Winter Games.

"Wow, you're the second person to ask me that today," I replied.

"Pull the disk out, I want you to look at it," he requested.

"I don't need to pull it out, I just saw it," I told him.

"Seriously, go get the disk," he replied.

Annoyed with his request, I pulled out my disk box only to discover that Winter Games was gone!

Turns out, Beach Boy's friend had not only swiped my disk, but had then bragged to Beach Boy about it, who told one of his friends, who told someone else who told Arcane. All of this happened during my drive home from the copyfest. You can say what you want about the speed of the Internet, but news traveled pretty quickly back then too! I confronted Beach Boy and his friend about the disk but they denied it. That's okay though – I got another copy of the game a few weeks later, and I got even with Beach Boy.

Back then, "password security" was not the big buzzword it is today. Beach Boy was stupid enough to use the same password on both his own board and on Arcane's board, on which I had sysop access. I tried the password he used on Arcane's board on Daytona Beach and what do you know, it worked! For the next year or so I would log in as Beach Boy into his own board, wreaking havoc by randomly deleting files, posting garbage and reading his private mail. Good times. I'm not sure he ever figured out what was going on, and he eventually took his board offline due to "ongoing technical difficulties."

With The Boss' BBS permanently offline, I moved my operations to Arcane's BBS, The Ball of Confusion. He was glad to have the constant stream of incoming software, and I was glad to have a place to conduct business.

The Boss' bust didn't deter any of us from pirating software; in fact, if anything, it made us realize that the authorities really weren't concerned about piracy at all. To them, the BBS scene was a virtual world, and the crimes committed within that world did not affect the real world. Credit card fraud did. We figured as long as we kept our activities within out own little virtual world and didn't cross over into theirs, nobody would care about what we were up to.

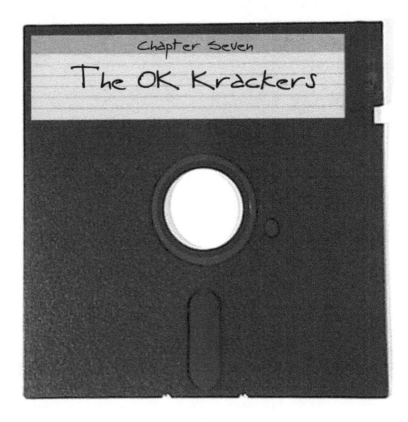

Chapter Seven

The OK Krackers

Klatu was one of the few people I'd met online who owned more programs than I did. Like myself, Klatu considered himself more of a librarian and software collector than a just a simple gamer. If I had 500 disks of games by then, he had 1,000. Between the two of us, we had probably the two largest Commodore software collections in the area. Both of us were calling long distance boards to acquire new programs by then. In fact, when Klatu upgraded to a newer modem, I purchased his old 2400 baud modem – a lightning fast piece of hardware for the Commodore 64 when one considers that the C64's serial bus couldn't even move information that fast. The price for that beauty? $350, complete with a RS-232 interface.

The more time Klatu and I spent talking the more I realized we were both doing the same thing; supplying Oklahoma City's Commodore boards with new software and not getting any credit for doing so! Most of the flow of new Commodore software was being brought into the area by just a few of us. One day Klatu expressed some interest in starting a project, one that would both keep the software flowing into Oklahoma and start giving us some credit for doing so. That project would evolve into the OK Krackers, or OKK for short (every good group had a three-letter abbreviation).

Klatu came up with the name and idea for OKK. The concept was simple; by coming up with our own group, we would begin getting credit for all the work, time and money and we were investing in bringing software to the local scene. The one problem we foresaw was, getting that credit might work against us as well; local users might start mobbing us for software, or worse, all this attention might put us on the local authorities' radar. We decided that we needed to go underground for this project and pick alternate personalities for the project. Klatu became Paladin, I became Metallica, and together we became the OK Krackers.

The first few releases by OKK were, by anyone's standard, lame. The first things we released were simply games that other people had cracked, but that no one in Oklahoma had seen. Back then, when a group "cracked" a game (removed its copy protection), they would add an intro screen to the front of the program. Everyone loading that game would get to watch the cracking group's intro screen before playing the game. Along with crackers there were also couriers, the people who officially spread software for cracking groups. Couriers were allowed to add a second intro screen to a game as well. People who added trainers (cheats) or converted a game's video mode from the European PAL format to the US NTSC standard also added intro screens. We decided if all these people got to add their screens to the fronts of games, no one would notice one more. Soon, the OK Krackers were adding their own "brought to you by" intros on the front of games as well. And technically, we *did* bring the games to Oklahoma City. In retrospect it seems kind of lame, but at least people began to realize where all the new games in our area were coming from. The sudden flush of games released by OKK got the attention of local modemers very quickly.

The first game OKK actually cracked on our own was Battle Chess, which used a very simple form of copy protection. Before the game started, Battle Chess asked you to complete a move from a historical game of chess. The answers to those moves were found within the game's paper manual – the thought process being that in order for you to play the game, you needed a copy of the game manual. If the game asked, "what was the winning move in the 1957 World Championship chess game?" you would type A4A2 or something like that. By sifting through the game's code manually, Klatu found the area on the disk where all the answers to all the questions were stored and changed them all to read "OKK!" (We needed the exclamation point so that our code would be four letters in length, just like the original codes were.) Then we slapped an intro onto the front of the game explaining to players that no matter what question the game asked you, the answer would be "OKK!". At that point people really began to stand up and take notice of the OK Krackers.

The third member of the OK Krackers was a mutual friend of ours who went by Bran Mac Morn. Bran was a programming genius and a whiz at cracking copy protection – and by that I don't mean using prefab tools or instructions that other people had written, I mean the guy could scroll through machine language code and figure out how to crack programs. Whenever we came across an original game that needed cracking, someone would immediately drive the disk out to Bran's house. I sat at his house one time and watched over his shoulder as the guy skimmed through assembly code faster than you or I could read plain English. It was amazing to watch and he was a definite asset to the crew.

The two brothers who ran The Enterprise BBS (Riker and Picard) actually lived on the same street as Klatu. The Enterprise was one of the few Commodore 64 boards I remember that actually had a hard drive, which was an expensive luxury back then. 20 Meg hard drives sold for $799. 40 Megs would set you back $1199. While 20 megabytes might not sound like much, it translated to hundreds of C64 floppy disks. Due to Klatu's relationship with the boys, The Enterprise BBS became the official home of the OK Krackers. Eventually Klatu purchased the board's hardware from the boys, and the board was relocated to Klatu's home where it was renamed The Warez Shop BBS. (We never were much for subtlety.) With that acquisition, the OK Krackers had one of the largest and most popular bulletin boards in town with all the latest programs. The board was so busy that even I had a difficult time logging on! Callers begged us for software, begged us to reveal our true identities and begged us to become members of the OK Krackers. Soon, we would add three more members.

OKK's fourth and fifth members were a couple of guys named Beetlejuice and 8-Ball. I was 15 years old when the OK Krackers' popularity skyrocketed. Klatu was a mailman in his 40s. Beetlejuice and 8-Ball lived on their own in an apartment with beer bottles everywhere, both having just turned 21 years old. Beetlejuice had a real knack for getting new software. He was calling lots of long distance BBSes

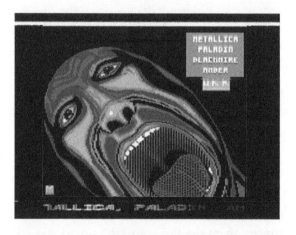

Various OKK Crack/Intro Screens

at the time, and judging by the state of his other finances I'm guessing he wasn't doing it legally. You never knew when Beetlejuice's phone would be cut off, or his electricity, or his water, or any other utility. He had a car that ran occasionally and he always seemed to be in between jobs. He was wild, fun, and unpredictable. To be honest I can't remember why we let 8-Ball join OKK other than the fact that he was a friend of Beetlejuice's. Looking back I'm glad we did. Not only did those two guys like computers, but they also liked to party; and more importantly, they liked to share their beer with minors such as myself.

Beetlejuice announced that he and 8-Ball would be throwing an all night computer party in honor of the OK Krackers, and all the OKK members as well as tons of other scene members were invited. Beetlejuice promised there would be lots of girls and beer for everyone.

My parents were pretty used to me going to computer parties at the time, and somehow I convinced them to let me go to this one. I'm sure they had no idea what was going to transpire that night or they wouldn't have let me within ten city blocks of that apartment. Heck, not even I knew what was in store that night.

My mom dropped me off at Beetlejuice's apartment around 6pm. I showed up with my Commodore computer, disk drive, and disks in tow, truly expecting a "computer" type party. Once I entered the apartment, I began to realize what I was in for. First of all, there was no other computer equipment in sight. The apartment's walls were completely white, save for a few holes punched in them here and there. A pyramid of beer cans sat stacked neatly in the front windowsill. The living room was completely devoid of furniture, save for the large pool table that sat in the middle of the room. True to his word, there were girls and beer everywhere. I remember Klatu showed up and stayed fifteen minutes, tops.

Once the party began rolling, Beetlejuice began complaining that there simply weren't enough girls there. Somehow he talked me into going to Cactus Jack's (the local arcade) with him to pick up even more girls. Beetlejuice and I piled into his MGB and drove over to Cactus Jack's. Once inside, Beetlejuice turned on the charm. He talked to every girl in sight, telling everyone about his party. Before long another five or six girls were on their way back to his apartment, all of them piled on top of Beetlejuice and me in his tiny two-seater convertible.

By the time we got back to his apartment, all hell was breaking loose. Someone had broken the apartment's front window with a wild billiards shot. People were running around everywhere (some clothed, some not) while yelling and screaming and dancing and chasing one another. It looked just like the wild party scene from Animal House. Before long someone walked by and stuck a beer in my hand. Not knowing what else to do, I drank it. Then I drank a couple more, egged on by the cheers of the crowd. I think I drank a total of twelve beers that night, which is a dumb idea for any fifteen-year-old's first foray into the world of alcohol consumption.

Around midnight there was a knock at the door. It was the police. At this point I was simply trying to go to sleep under the pool table, or maybe on top of it. I remember the cops wanting to know what the hell was going on and them telling Beetlejuice that he was in a lot of trouble. I knew that if I got caught drinking I would be too, and not just by the police. The police began dividing the group into people over 21 and those under 21. All the minors were sent into the back bedroom while everyone of legal age was asked to come to the living room. I stumbled into the bedroom, and immediately my fight or flight reflexes kicked in. Once the bedroom door was shut I opened the window, pushed out the screen, and dove out onto the ground below. Beetlejuice's apartment sat on a slope, and so I dropped four or five feet out onto the sidewalk below, landing on my shoulder. Looking for a place to run to, I noticed a used car lot next door. I ran to the car lot and tried opening a couple of different car doors. They were all locked. Fortunately for me, this was before the era of car alarms. After giving up on finding an unlocked car, I hopped into the bed of a pickup for sale, and fell fast asleep.

I woke myself up shivering. Without a watch, I had no idea what time it was. I crawled over the bed of the truck and stumbled back to the apartment. My arm was scraped and bleeding from the fall and my shirt was wet from water sitting in the truck's bed.

"What the hell happened to you?" Beetlejuice said when he answered the door. While I had been hiding for over two hours, the police had only been at the apartment for less than five minutes and had basically just told everyone to quiet down. Beetlejuice told me I looked like I should go lie down, and I agreed. In the corner of his bedroom sat a black, vinyl foldout chair. My last memory of that night is throwing up on that black vinyl chair, and then lying face down in it to go to sleep.

"Wake up dude, your mom's here."

I pried open one eye. The other was stuck shut with dried puke, which was not only in my eye but also in my hair, on my face, and on the chair, which my hair was now stuck to. I could tell it was morning by the sunlight peering in through the blinds.

After peeling my face off the black vinyl, I began collecting my things and carrying them out to my mother's van. Neither of us said anything on the ride home. My guess is by the looks of my ripped shirt, scraped shoulder, bloodied arm and puked on clothes, she figured I had already learned suffered enough. I do distinctly remember that that was the last time I was ever allowed to visit Beetlejuice's apartment.

Despite drunken debauchery, the OK Krackers marched on. Eventually, another friend of Klatu's named Mysteria was added to our clan's roster. I don't think she ever did anything for the group on any technical level, and was simply added because she was Klatu's friend. Plus, adding another member made the OK Krackers look even bigger and more mysterious than we really were.

One of my favorite OKK stories involved Doc Dred. Doc Dred was a long-standing enemy of both Klatu and myself, although it's been so long I can't exactly remember why. I remember at one point in time the two of us had modified a pretty graphic homosexual picture and made a demo out of it called "Dick Dred." Legend has it that Doc Dred got so angry about it that he actually made a copy of it and took it to the local police department to lodge an indecency complaint against us. I don't know if he really did or not, but the thought of it at the time really made us laugh.

Mysteria was a bit of a double agent for OKK. Not only was she a friend of Klatu's, but a friend of Doc Dred and his group of friends as well. Through a friend of a friend, Mysteria ended up with a copy of Doc Dred's bulletin board software. For Klatu and me, this was a goldmine. For starters, with this software we were able to retrieve all his users' personal information, including their real names, phone numbers, addresses and passwords. While I enjoyed playing with his users' information, Klatu had an even more diabolical plan in store. His idea was to strip all of Doc Dred's information out of the BBS software and release the program as an OKK release! After a day or so of work, we slapped an OKK tag on the program and began uploading it all over town. This ended up being even funnier than we had originally planned. Doc Dred, hell-bent on getting the OK Krackers busted, contacted the authors of the BBS software and informed them that we had released a pirated copy of their software. The authors of the software informed him that if he could provide a copy of the release, they would look in to the matter. More importantly, from that release they could determine who had originally purchased (and therefore leaked) the program. Imagine Doc Dred's surprise when he sent them what turned out to be a copy of his OWN BBS software! Mysteria relayed the proceedings back to us. We must've laughed for weeks about that.

Although it resulted in a fairly uneventful relationship, it is interesting to note that through the OK Krackers I got my first groupie, who ended up being my first official girlfriend. Her name was Liz, and she went by Christian Hosoi online. Christian Hosoi is a guy's name (he was a famous skater in the 1980s), so when Liz originally mailed me about "hanging out sometime," I had assumed that she was a he. Not so. Liz sent me a lot of messages asking me questions about the OK Krackers – so many, in fact, that I was a bit suspicious as to her motives. They ended up being benign. She just wanted to date a "member of the scene" she once told me. How utterly ridiculous.

The two of us hung out at a local amusement park, the fair, and a few modem parties. I was old enough to drive and she was not, so our dates always began with me pulling into her driveway to pick her up. Her mom never cared for me much. After a while our dates began with me calling Liz and giving her a ten minute's notice, then parking down the street at the local elementary school and having her meet me there.

Our relationship ended with as much passion as it had begun with – not much. A few months after we began dating, I picked up two tickets to see Faith No More, her favorite band at the time. The night of the concert, I called Liz's house. Her mom answered the phone, told me that Liz had gone out with a bunch of her friends, and that I was not to call there anymore.

Later I found out that Liz had in fact been sitting at home that night, waiting for me to pick her up. She was so distraught over the whole ordeal that she (according to her) attempted suicide.

It eventually dawned on me that suicidal modem chicks pretending to be boys online and possessing crazy mothers might not be ideal suitors. I quit calling whatever board I met her on and eventually she and her crazy family went away.

For the next couple of years, the OK Krackers did what they did best; find, crack, and release software. We all fell into our roles. Bran Mac Morn cracked anything we sent his direction. Klatu ran the BBS and served as the group's backbone. I performed PR and served as the mouth of the group. Klatu, Beetlejuice, 8-Ball and I continued to move files in and out of the area code as needed. Eventually the true identities of the OK Krackers leaked, but by the time word got out it didn't matter much. Due to advances in technology and newer computer systems, the Commodore scene had begun to die.

Chapter Eight

Death and Rebirth

The Commodore 64 really began to show its age during my high school years in the early 90s. Commodore's Amiga had surpassed the C64's graphic and sound abilities half a decade earlier. Macintosh and Atari also had computers that could easily outperform my beloved C64; however, I hardly knew anyone who owned any of those machines. Most home computer owners were hedging their bets on the IBM platform, which is what most businesses and schools were rapidly moving to. The problem was, IBM PCs couldn't play games better than a Commodore 64 could – at least not in the beginning.

Early PC games utilized CGA video, which ran at 320x200 resolution (the same as a Commodore) but could only display 4 colors at a time versus the 64's 16 colors. But throughout the late 80s and early 90s IBM's hardware began to rapidly mature. By the late 80s most PCs could perform in VGA mode (640x480 with sixteen simultaneous on-screen colors). PC audio began to advance as well; Creative Labs' Sound Blaster line of soundcards gave the IBM a much-needed audio upgrade. Prior to that, PC sounds came from your internal speaker. With these new soundcards, external speakers and microphones could be easily connected to your PC.

And that was the beauty of the PC's design. Video cards, sound cards, and memory upgrades were being released at mind-blowing speeds – and as fast as bigger and better parts were released, you could purchase them off the shelf and upgrade your home computer by yourself. The Commodore 64 simply couldn't compete with IBM's open-architecture design. There was no mass-market solution to upgrading your Commodore's processor, or the amount of RAM, or basically anything. There were a few add-ons here and there that were supposed to increase performance, but without widespread adoption no one was willing to program software to take advantage of them.

The final nail on the coffin was Microsoft's Windows operating system. The Commodore's GEOS operating system was a nice attempt, but running a GUI off a floppy disk that was notoriously slow to begin with never caught on with the masses. As mice began replacing keyboards as computer operator's input device of choice, Commodore computers began slowly fading from the public eye.

While I still considered myself a Commodore user, I was also quite familiar with the IBM PC. I had been using a PC since my dad had purchased one three or four years earlier. I kept my C64 around for games, but the PC was great for word processing and such.

After opting out of my high school's BASIC programming class (which was still being taught on TRS-80 Model III machines), I enrolled in my first official computer course my senior year of high school in 1990: General Computing. The yearlong class was divided up into four nine-week sections: word processing, spreadsheets, databases, and general computer knowledge. By 1990 I had been using computers for a solid ten years; half of that time had been spent running a very large and well-organized piracy ring from the confines of my bedroom. I needed basic computer education like I needed a hole in the head, but it was either that or physical education, and sitting in a room full of computers sounded like a lot more fun than sitting in room full of sweaty dudes doing sit-ups.

In General Computing I ended up sitting next to a guy named The Stranger. The Stranger's father worked for Xerox, so their family had owned a PC for several years. I knew of The Stranger as a friend of a friend, a guy who hung around with other people I knew, but I didn't really know he was into computers until we ended up in class together. It turns out The Stranger was a fellow modemer as well.

Try to imagine sitting through a basic beginner's course on anything you've been doing for the past ten years: driving a car, perhaps. Then imagine yourself stuck in a room with 20 other people who have never driven or even seen a car before, being led by a teacher who is there to teach *everybody else* how to drive. This was the hell The Stranger and I found ourselves stuck in. Here sat Jack Flack and The Stranger in a room full of people who didn't even know how to use a mouse. I distinctly remember an assignment that involved using a typing tutor program. Each student had to be able to get the program up to 20-words-per-minute before they could leave class that day. The Stranger and I had a contest to see who could get the program up over 100-words-per-minute. As you can imagine, we spent several days in that classroom bored out of our skulls, and it didn't take long before we began finding ways to entertain ourselves.

Our teacher's first name was Mary Jo and around that same time I had read a book about circus freaks, one of which was Jo-Jo The Dog Faced Boy. Somehow the two got mixed together and we began referring to the teacher (behind her back, of course) as Jojo. Jojo was also the LAN (Local Area Network) Administrator of our school's network. The computers in the office, library and our classroom were all networked together using Novell. The Stranger and I didn't really understand Novell or networking, but we were both extremely familiar with DOS and could get around on the network (at least the parts we had access to) with ease. The network had a couple of shared drives that all students had access to. There was a directory full of programs that was read-only, and then each student had a home directory that he or she had read/write access to. This allowed us to run programs from the network and save our homework in our home directories, but not share files between students. At least, that was the intention.

Although The Stranger and I didn't know much about networks, we understood the concept that the teacher had more access than we did. The two of us sat near the front of the class, and had watched Jojo add new users to the network before. A plan was devised that was decidedly both low-tech and risky. We decided to wait for the teacher to leave the classroom; when she did, we would create our own administrator account. As stupid as the plan sounded, it worked. One day during class, Jojo was called to the office. When she left, I simply walked up to her computer and created a new account:

I don't remember where the idea for password came from, other than it rhymed with Jojo and would be easy to remember. It must've been; fifteen years later, I still remember it!

Once we had admin rights, we immediately went to work on the network. We had no intention of deleting any files or tearing anything up – we were far less destructive than kids these days. Our goal was simple: copy games to the network, where we (and maybe our friends) could play them later.

Copying the games up was a straightforward procedure. As I mentioned, Novell accepted all the DOS commands we were already familiar with. The Stranger and I would sneak our favorite games (stored on floppy disks) into the library. From there, we would create directories for our games and copy the files up into them. When finished, we would use the DOS ATTRIB command to hide the directories and files. Even we couldn't see them – you just had to know where they were to be able to play the games.

Most PC games back then fit on a single 3 ½ disk, so bringing games to and from school was not a problem. Prince of Persia, Rogue, and Indy 500 were three of our favorites. We began getting so many games on the network that we began to lose track of what was where. Eventually, I wrote a simple menu batch file that would allow students to pick and play the game of their choice.

Yes, I said students. For a while, only The Stranger and I had access to the game directory, but slowly I began telling other people about our creation.

I'm not really sure how we got caught, but we did. The first thing to disappear was our JOJO account. One day it simply quit working. A few days later, my teacher and I had one of those "anonymous" conversations. She asked me if I had any idea who might have created an admin account. I told her that I didn't know who had done it, but if I had known, I'm sure it was created as a learning tool and that nothing malicious was done with it. She then said she was glad, because if something bad were to happen the network she had a pretty good idea who to come to. She smiled, I smiled, and that was that. A few weeks later, I managed to get a second admin account set up. I was a little smarter that time, and named it to resemble a student's name. Using that account, I moved the games to another location that only The Stranger and I knew about, and kept our mouths shut about it. The games (and the account) remained undetected on the network for the remainder of the school year.

Throughout my senior year I continued to dabble in both the Commodore and PC worlds. Many of my friends had begun moving to the IBM platform, and it became more and more difficult to find people to trade Commodore programs with. Software always has been and always will be the name of the game. Without software, computers become really expensive paperweights; the fun is where the games are. My sources began rapidly drying up. During the summer of '91, many Commodore-dedicated bulletin boards disappeared. We were being squeezed out of the game.

The "game" I soon discovered, follows the software trail. PC games began taking advantage of their advanced hardware. PC games began actually looking and sounding good! PC hard drives made games run faster than ever before and eliminated disk swapping. It was an exciting time.

As I said goodbye to my high school friends, I began to say goodbye to my Commodore 64 as well. For years all I did on my computer was collect software. Now, it sat collecting dust.

Throughout my senior year I continued to dabble in both the Commodore and PC worlds. Many of my friends had begun moving to the IBM platform, and it became more and more difficult to find people to trade Commodore programs with. Software always has been and always will be the name of the game. Without software, computers become really expensive paperweights; the fun is where the games are. My sources began rapidly drying up. During the summer of '91, many Commodore-dedicated bulletin boards disappeared. We were being squeezed out of the game.

For the next couple of years I took a much-needed vacation from the world of computers. Just months after graduating from high school I enrolled at Redlands Community College (RCC) and began working toward an associate's degree in Journalism. Had I known that two-year degree was going to take me ten years to achieve, I might have taken school a bit more seriously back then.

Redlands' journalism department was the first place I worked with Macintosh computers. Several times we were told how state of the art our journalism lab filled with Macintosh Plus computers was. A bunch of tiny computers with nine-inch black-and-white screens didn't seem very cutting edge to me at the time. Still, the machines were powerful enough to run PageMaker, which we used to layout our school's newspaper. It didn't take long before I was doing most of the journalism department's computer work. Kelly Rupp, head of RCC's Journalism department, was computer savvy as well. Between the two of us, we were able to figure out everything we needed to do.

Kelly Rupp recognized my writing and computer talents right away and put me to work, literally. As a freshman in college I was made the editor of the school's yearbook, and served on the staff of the school's newspaper as well, doing the layout and design for both. My sophomore year, I took over as the editor of both publications. By then, Kelly had actually hired me through the school, paying me 300 bucks a month for both editorial positions.

Leap of Faith (Journalism Class, 1992)

My two best friends that year were a couple of guys named Chebon and Jim. All three of us had completely off-the-wall and twisted senses of humor, so the entire year became a series of in-jokes and laughter. One of the things we were constantly doing was writing top ten lists. "The top ten things you don't want to hear while flying." "The top ten things to do when the world's about to end." "The top ten signs you may be an alien." These lists kept us entertained to no end. Of course half of the items on our lists would be in-jokes and things that only the three of us would find funny in the first place. Chebon was also big into music (as am I), so we were constantly turning each other on to both new and old bands. Chebon introduced me to Led Zeppelin and Ministry; I introduced him to Cypress Hill and Nine Inch Nails.

The three of us, along with Kelly, spent a lot of a time both in and out of school together. Chebon and Jim ended up becoming our paper's head photographers, so the four of us spent many weekends together hanging out in the journalism lab working together. All of us became really good friends with Kelly, who stuck up for a bunch of slackers more than she probably should have. In one edition of our paper, we published an investigative article focusing on underage drinking, specifically focusing on RCC's FFA students. The following weekend, the FFA sponsor came up to the school looking for us to discuss the article. Unfortunately, I myself had ingested *way* too much alcohol the night before, and had shown up on a weekend to work completely plastered. Kelly basically propped me up in a corner as she did the computer layout herself and told me in no uncertain terms how pissed off at me she was. That was about the time the FFA professor showed up to talk with Kelly and me about our "underage drinking" article. Kelly defended the article the entire time, even though several times throughout the encounter I had to excuse myself from the room so I could step outside and throw up in the bushes.

I have no doubt that Chebon, Jim and I must've significantly raised Kelly's blood pressure levels, but to my knowledge I don't think we ever failed to meet a deadline. I'm sure we came close many times; in fact, we put the final touches on the 1992-1993 Redlands yearbook with only minutes to spare. But we made it. After two years of dealing with us, I think Kelly got used to our nutty behavior and late nights, and we got used to getting away with it. I'm sure had we missed a single deadline Kelly would have been all over us, but somehow we managed to narrowly escape disaster every deadline for two years straight.

And for those two years I attended 15 credit hours of school each semester, put in 20 hours a week at RCC for my editorial positions, *and* worked another 40 hours a week on top of that in various fast food restaurants. After two years of that routine, I was completely burned out on school and decided to quit before finishing my degree. As an alternative to college, my father offered me a job at the company he worked at, Oklahoma Graphics. What kid doesn't want to follow in his father's footsteps? Even though he warned me I'd be starting at the bottom and would get no special treatment, I readily accepted the offer, said goodbye to my friends at Redlands Community College, and began my new career as a "stacker."

RCC Journalism Staff. Chebon, 2nd from left (back row). Kelly Rupp, 4th from left (back row). Jim Bear, far right. I'm the one in the front wearing shorts and a flannel shirt (Redlands, 1993).

Oklahoma Graphics (which has since closed) was a huge printing company. The C-700 printing press I worked on was a hundred feet long and stood two stories high. The rolls of paper it used weighed over a ton each, and when operating at full speed the press could print over 50,000 books an hour. My pressroom specialized in ad circulars (the type you might find in your Sunday newspaper or lying in your shopping cart). Oklahoma Graphics printed jobs for companies like Wal-Mart and Home Depot, sometimes running millions of books each week for those customers.

My first day of work consisted of being shown all the moving parts on the press that could kill me, which turned out to be quite a few. At one end of the press was that huge roll of paper I mentioned. The paper webbed through ink rollers, blankets, ovens, chiller rolls, razor-sharp cutting blades, folding units and joggers before they ended up at the other end, where I stood. For twelve hours a day, three days a week, my job was to stack the books onto pallets as they came off the end of the press. Hence the name "stacker."

There were no breaks, and meals were to be brought and eaten while you stacked. In my mind, all that was missing was somebody with horns, a pitchfork, and red leotards.

I had wanted to get away from the mental challenges of college and I had gotten my wish. For twelve hours a day I stacked books onto wooden slats. My three days a week turned into four when we began working Sundays. Even more disheartening was when another stacker would take vacation. When that happened, I'd have to work Sunday, then my three days, then *their* three days, *their* Sunday, and then *my* three days again, turning my three day work week into eleven straight days. The job was so physically demanding that I would fall asleep the minute I got home and would wake up just in time to make it back to work. The paychecks were great but the routine got old in a hurry.

After working at Oklahoma Graphics for three months (and losing 35 pounds in the process), I received a phone call from an old high school sweetheart named Susan. Susan had moved to Weatherford, Oklahoma (exactly 60 miles west of where we had gone to high school) to attend college. Her mother had purchased a three-bedroom mobile home for Susan to live in while she was attending college, and Susan was looking for two roommates. She couldn't have had better timing. I must've given my two weeks notice within seconds of receiving that phone call. I don't know if it was my father's intention to show me what the world of physical labor was like by hiring me, but if it was it worked.

On August 22nd, 1993 (my 20th birthday), I packed up all my stuff (including my trusty Commodore 64) and moved in with Susan. Our other roommate was a girlfriend of Susan's named Holly (who turned out to be a depressed, psychotic fruitcake who drank to the point of passing out, both needed and attended therapy, and slept with a gun under her pillow to protect her from God knows what.)

Susan and I had sorta-kinda dated in high school but hadn't talked much over the two years since. In her mind, by moving into the trailer we were now dating one another exclusively and were on the road to getting married. She just, you know, neglected to tell *me* that at the time. Sneaky girls.

Our trailer had three bedrooms, and I got the master bedroom (which was on one end of the trailer) and my own bathroom all to myself, while the girls got the smaller kids bedrooms (located at the other end of the trailer) and shared the other bathroom. As I moved my things and furniture into the house, I felt really empty without having a computer there. Within a couple of days of living in the trailer I had unpacked my old Commodore and set it up it on my old computer desk in my bedroom. I don't know that I ever turned it on or even connected all the wires, but the place just didn't feel like home without having a computer sitting on the other side of the room staring back at me – even if the computer in question was severely underpowered and outdated.

Girls in love sometimes do stupid things for guys they are in love with. Shortly after the semester began, Susan's mom mailed her a blank check, which was supposed to be used for paying Susan's tuition. Don't ask me how this happened, but somehow I talked her into buying me a new computer with the check instead. A friend of mine from school named Josh worked at a local computer store assembling computers. 486 processors (the chip before the Pentium) had dropped in price, which meant I (with the help of a blank check) could finally afford a 386. Josh told me to pay for the parts I could afford and he would float me the ones I couldn't. For about $600 I got a monitor, a tower, and a motherboard. Josh floated me RAM and a hard drive that worked most of the time. I think my first keyboard and mouse were actually stolen from the school's computer lab.

After purchasing the computer parts, I spent the weekend at Josh's dad's place assembling the beast. My dad taught me so much about how computers worked, but it was Josh who first showed me how to assemble a PC. Step by step I worked my way through the machine, adding the memory, connecting the wires and tightening every screw myself. We copied programs late into the night using Laplink. "Laplink Cables" were a popular way to connect two machines together. Instead of copying hundreds of floppies (and computer CD-Roms were unheard of), you could connect two computers using a Laplink cable (which connected computers' parallel ports, essentially creating a poor man's network) and copy files from one to another. Laplink wasn't fast. Josh and I stayed up until the wee hours of the morning waiting for the files to finish copying, while Susan had crashed hours before on Josh's couch.

I spent the next couple of months learning that machine inside and out. I was obsessed with knowing everything it could possibly do.

Susan and I decided to spend the Christmas of 1993 at my dad's house back in Yukon. In the few short months that I had owned an IBM, I found myself getting addicted to computers all over again. I decided that I could not live without my PC for a whole week so I stuck the whole thing in Susan's trunk and brought it to my dad's with me.

On Christmas morning when everyone began exchanging presents, I realized that I had remembered to bring my computer but had forgot Susan's Christmas present. And make no mistake; she was *not* happy about it. We eventually smoothed things over, but if I remember correctly it took a lot of flowers.

Once again, I was addicted.. Through my prestigious pseudo-management position at Long John Silver's I scraped up enough money to purchase both a modem and a soundcard for my computer. Using the modem I had begun calling bulletin boards all over the state once again. There were very few bulletin boards that were free to call from the Weatherford area, so I had resorted to using watts extenders, calling cards (which I traded software to get), and any other method I could come up with to circumvent paying for long distance phone charges. The need to be online constantly was stronger than any logic or fear of getting caught. We had a computer at work that dialed fish headquarters (or whatever) nightly to report our daily sales; I installed my terminal dialing software on *that* computer and started calling long distance boards during work hours. One time I screwed up my computer at home and found myself stuck without a copy of Windows to reinstall. I remembered that next to the computer at work we had a stack of recovery floppies, so the next night I brought the stack of disks home and used them to reload my computer. For the next year or so, every time my machine booted up I had to look at a custom Long John Silver's loading screen.

There's no doubt that the amount of time I was spending on my computer in combination with the long hours I was spending at Long John Silver's contributed to the grades I was earning. I had only completed nine credit hours in the fall semester, and was well on my way to failing every class I had enrolled in that spring. My journalism professor dealt me my final blow of the semester. I showed up to class one day and found all of my personal items had been removed from my editor's desk and were waiting for me in a cardboard box. I had been fired from my positions as the school's yearbook editor and as a section editor of the school's newspaper. My professor was in tears, claiming that despite the fact I was a great writer, my erratic schedule and lack of dedication to the journalism program were literally giving her ulcers. And what could I say? She was right. My professor told me she had picked a replacement for me, and wanted me to spend some time with her the next day passing on information. I gathered my things and said I would.

That was the last time I ever stepped in that classroom.

That night I told Susan what had happened. I was too ashamed and embarrassed to return to school and face those people again. Susan, the ever practical one, thought we should buckle down, quit our jobs, and try to pull out at least a few passing grades that semester. As she was saying this, I pulled a quarter out of my pocket.

"Heads, we do just that," I said.

"And what if it's tails?" she asked.

Wanting to get away from everything, the first thing that came out of my mouth was "well, I've always wanted to see the Grand Canyon." I flipped the quarter high into the air, and it landed tails side up.

"So now what?" Susan asked.

"I guess we pack our bags," I said. And just like that, we began packing for our road trip. We would depart at dawn. But first, I had to make a phone call.

"Dad? Yeah, this is Rob. Oh fine, fine. Listen, I have a quick question for you. How do you get to the Grand Canyon?"

"Go west," he replied. "You'll find it."

He was right. After a couple of days of driving west, we eventually found the Grand Canyon. Along the way we stopped at several other sites, including Carlsbad Caverns, Meteor Crater, Old

Rob at Cadillac Ranch … (1994)

…and living dangerously at the Grand Canyon (1994)

Tucson, Cadillac Ranch and Bedrock City, USA. Susan and I took a ton of pictures during that week and will always remember the great time we had. Meanwhile, back in Weatherford, Oklahoma, finals week was taking place. Without us.

When we got home from our road trip the reality of our situation began to set in. We had flunked out of school, quit our jobs and spent all our money within the same week. With no reason to remain in Weatherford, we made a deal with Susan's mom to have the mobile home moved back home to Oklahoma City. That was the easiest move ever. All we had to do was take our stuff off of shelves and put it on the floor. Then the moving company showed up, put wheels on our mobile home, towed it to its new destination and removed the wheels. Instant relocation!

The next six months were, with no offense to Dickens, both the best and worst of times. For months, Susan and I remained jobless. At times, the two of us would sneak over to my dad's house at night and raid his kitchen cabinets for food while he was at work. Eventually, Susan's mom offered us jobs at her budding BBQ restaurant. The five bucks per hour pay wasn't nearly as important as the access to free meat. For months we lived off of Ramen Noodles and BBQ. We worked a few hours a day and played the rest.

The good news was, that loose schedule afforded me lots of computer time. Soon, empires would be both built and destroyed, wars would be launched, and lots and lots of mischief would be had.

Jack Flack was back in town.

Rob "BBQ Pig" O'Hara and Susan. (1994)

Chapter Nine

TBH405

Infiltrating and dominating the local IBM PC underground scene was relatively simple, as I'd already been through the process several times before in both the Apple and Commodore 64 worlds. But in the PC world, things were a bit different. Part of the difference could be attributed to the explosion of the home computer market. Back when Commodore and Apple ruled the land, computer owners were generally computer enthusiasts, either young teens who had scammed their parents into believing that a Commodore 64 could somehow improve their grades, or adults who played with computers as a hobby. Trading pirated software was commonplace among both of those demographics. But by the early 90s, computers were no longer rare commodities. Even people who wouldn't consider themselves "computer people" began purchasing computers. Images of businessmen with big clunky IBM PCs in their homes were plastered everywhere in print and television ads. The message they conveyed was clear: anybody who wanted to be someone in the workforce needed a home computer! As the number of computer owners climbed, many of them became interested in the local modem scene and began to put their own BBSes online. But unlike the Commodore world I was familiar with, many of these "legitimate" bulletin boards did not condone the pirating of software. But, just like on the old Commodore boards, it was pretty simple to differentiate between legit and underground boards simply by their names.

While the Commodore had always been looked upon as a kid's toy, IBM was big business, which also meant big trouble and big fines if you (somehow) got busted for pirating software. Hell, among my old Commodore friends it was rare to find someone who *didn't* copy software. Many IBM users were reluctant to admit openly that they illegally copied software.

More and more pirate bulletin boards began going underground. Many of these boards looked legit but had private back rooms for file swapping. Access to these private areas was usually granted to friends, and later friends of friends. Personally, I rarely had the patience or the time to get involved in these private groups. There were so many bulletin boards out there blatantly offering illegal software that it seemed counterproductive to spend months trying to get into some "inner circle" of old farts who almost certainly had less software sources than myself.

Blatant pirate boards began adding NUPs, or New User Passwords. When you connected to one of these boards you would be required to supply a password before you were allowed to log in or even apply. On really private systems, these passwords could change on a monthly or even weekly basis.

As I began calling PC bulletin boards, I slipped back into old habits easily. It was less like reinventing the wheel and more like simply transferring to a new school. Building a software collection was a simple matter of finding a few people with software and acting as a middleman, working out trades between them and retaining copies of everything that passed through my hands.

As I continued to call more and more pirate boards, I began to see the same names time and time again, working the same circles I was. These were the people who would become the basis of the 405 scene in the very near future.

Unlike Internet communities that are often comprised of people who have never met one another, it was not uncommon for people to meet each other in person back in the BBS days. Since we were all calling the same local bulletin boards, it stood to reason that we all lived relatively close to one another. Many boards were known for their "BBS parties", where fellow modem geeks would gather to party hard (as only geeks can). It wasn't long before I was invited to my first one in the PC world.

If you think walking into a school dance or work party is awkward, imagine entering a party full of people you've never even met in real life before. No matter how many times you do it, it's always weird since meeting people you have spoken with online but whose face you have never seen. Some of the people at these parties even preferred to be referred to by their online alias instead of their real name. There's nothing like politely shaking hands with someone who has just introduced himself to you as "Dragonspit." Of course, we soon found that all those jitters weren't anything that couldn't be overcome with a little alcohol

The first PC modem party I attended was called "The Gathering," and was co-hosted by Rivas J'Kara (his idea) and Flagg (his apartment). I hadn't met either of them prior to the party, but I *did* know FalseGod, who was friends with Blackcloud, who was friends with Gatoperro, who was friends with Rivas. I think. That's how these things worked. Rivas dubbed the party "The Gathering" in homage to the great European demo parties, known as "Assemblies."

After arriving at the party I made the rounds, meeting many people that I'd been chatting with online for over a year in person for the first time. Ozzymandias sat against a wall with a watermelon in his lap that had a bottle of vodka stuck in it. Occasionally he'd pull the bottle out of the watermelon, take a swig from the bottle, and stick it back in the melon. Next to him quietly sat Violetta Kitten, a gothic looking girl who was either too nervous or too cool to make much conversation with. Rivas, FalseGod and a few others were busy in the kitchen daring each other to drink strange and bizarre homemade drinks – the one I specifically remember watching them drink was the "half Jack Daniels, half Pace Picante Sauce" concoction. A particularly loud kid named Ghost in the Machine (GitM) walked around the party explaining to anyone who would listen why his hand was bandaged up. Fellow Long John Silver's alumni GitM had cut his hand at work, bled into the coleslaw he was preparing, and served it to customers anyway. Interesting fellow.

Late into the party, a couple of guys named Yaun-Ti and Prong arrived. Yaun-Ti was a scruffy looking guy, his small frame making him appear much younger than he really was. His dirty blonde hair covered his eyes and he wore a frayed jean jacket. Prong was the muscle of the two, appearing more like a bodyguard than a pal. His cut off sleeves showed both the definition of his arms and the tattoos located thereon. The two characters demanded the room's attention.

FalseGod, Jack Flack and Anacodia (1998)

After a few minutes of making small talk, Yaun-Ti broke into a rambling diatribe about his views of the local scene. No one was working together, he lamented. In his vision, the elite users of Oklahoma City would unite to form an elite brotherhood. As it was common for modemers to proudly wear their area codes on their sleeve, the name "The Brotherhood of 405" was bandied around and later condensed to TBH405. TBH405 was to be a group of elite users who would bond together, essentially to help each other out. TBH405 consisted of artists, musicians, hackers, pirates … you name it, we had one. I was originally recruited because of my software connections. Just like that The Brotherhood of 405 had officially been formed, and I was a charter member.

Pinning down exactly what TBH405 was proved to be pretty difficult. In the beginning Yaun-Ti wouldn't even admit that an official member list existed. There was no application process, no charter and no real definition of who we were or what we were up to; we simply found users, sysops and bulletin boards that seemed like a good fit and assimilated them into the group. Soon we had a stable of members whose skills covered all the bases. Gatoperro provided ANSI graphics. From logos to signatures, the guy was constantly churning out good work. Yaun-Ti, aside from acting as ringleader, was also a very talented VGA artist. Buster Friendly (often referred to by me as Buster UN-Friendly and who later became Leperkhan) and Rivas were the group's resident coders. From viewers to demos these guys could whip out anything. FalseGod stayed busy directing traffic via several modem nets and was a central port of communication, while I kept the warez flowing in for everybody. My BBS became a central hub for 405 members to trade software. Eventually I added a second phone line exclusively for TBH405 members.

It should be mentioned that most of these people were involved in other groups and projects as well. Gatoperro and Yaun-Ti were both in the art group TiTAN; Gatoperro was a trial member of iCE for a while. I was running both Soulz at Zero and SiTH at the same time. FalseGod and Ghost in the Machine were writing PhaCT (another local 'zine). No Carrier was a courier for DWI and PiG, as were several other locals such as Hit Man, Chewbacca, and Pistol Pete. These scattered efforts were Yaun-Ti's biggest complaint about the 405 scene – too many people were working on too many different projects. His goal was to focus all of that energy into one local group. The only way to do that was to get organized and get the word out, and that was done through the official TBH405 Newsletters.

Yaun-Ti released the first issue of the TBH405 Newsletter on July 27, 1994. The first issue contained interviews with several local users who would later become TBH405 members along with several quotes from local scene members and references to underground boards. No phone numbers or new user passwords were ever given out in the newsletters, which stirred the local modem community into a frenzy. The first issue of the electronic newsletter simply consisted of a zip file that contained the newsletter in plain text format, one standalone VGA picture, and one ANSI art file. It wasn't until a few issues later that the group would get its own viewer (written by Rivas), replaced a few issues later by one written by Buster Friendly.

Yaun-Ti assembled each issue by himself, using writing submissions from several other TBH members. Once he had received "enough" (some unknown, magical number) submissions, Yaun-Ti would compile the text into the final product. Notice I said "compile" and not "edit" – spellcheckers be damned. Each issue contained tons of local gossip, interviews, scene news, reviews, and lots of pointed commentary and opinions. No two releases were alike. One might have software reviews while the next one might not. In skimming through the old issues I found several articles that were introduced as "part one of a multi-part article" which were never completed. Issues were usually both inconsistent and incongruent. And people loved them.

The words were crude and the editing was rough, but the message got out. The TBH405 newsletters became some of the hottest downloads. They were a newsletter, a gossip rag, and a recruiting tool rolled into one.

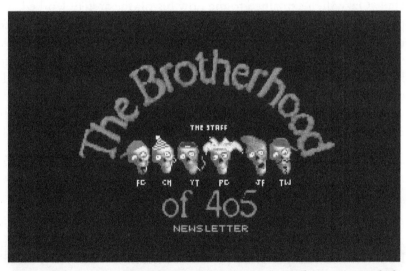

One of the many TBH405 viewer intro graphics. From left to right: FalseGod, Chewbacca, Yaun-Ti, Prong, Jack Flack and The Warlord.

As the popularity of TBH405 began to take off, it only made sense that there should be a Gathering II. A slightly pudgy hacker by the name of Ozzymandias offered up his tiny apartment as the location for the next gathering, and actually ended up hosting numbers II and III.

Ozzymandias was slightly less than normal, and I mean that in a good way. He was overweight, wore thick glasses, and had bad, wavy hair. I'm sure in school he would have hung out with either the geeks or the stoners, whichever group would have had him. Ozzy was also extremely funny, generous, and completely and certifiably insane. Anyone who ever hung out with Ozzy for more than a day or two had a story about something crazy he had done. At the Gathering III, Ozzy was either so stoned or so drunk (or both) that he passed out and fell into his living room wall, knocking his front tooth out. By the time I got to his side, he was sitting there smiling with a big bloody hole in his grin where his front tooth had formerly been. Someone later told me that they had found his tooth still sticking in the wall.

At one point during The Gathering II I asked Ozzy if I could use his phone. He said sure, and walked me over to his living room window. On the windowsill sat a phone with a phone line that ran out through the opening. Attached to the end of the phone cable was a pair of alligator clips. Ozzy then explained to me how his phone system worked. The phone box for Ozzy's entire apartment complex was mounted directly outside his apartment. To use the phone, Ozzy would lean out the window and attach the alligator clips to a random phone jack. Sometimes he would get a dead connection; other times he would break into the middle of someone's conversation. If you tried enough pairs eventually you would get a dial tone. I once asked Ozzy what he would do if he got caught and he simply shrugged his shoulders as if the concept itself was foreign to him. The man was fearless.

Both Gatherings held at Ozzy's apartment were huge successes. At the end of The Gathering III, Yaun-Ti became so drunk and belligerent that his girlfriend (now wife) left him at the party. I told Yaun-Ti not to worry about it; I'd take him home. Unfortunately for him, I was in no shape to drive either. Charon offered to do the driving, so the three of us piled into my father's pickup that I had borrowed for the night and headed off to Norman, Oklahoma, some forty-five minutes from where Ozzy lived. Yaun-Ti was so smashed out of his gourd that before we even got to the interstate he tried to open the truck door and get out – while we were driving! It was quickly decided that he should sit in the middle, with Charon and myself flanking him.

At some point during the drive I passed out, leaving Charon as the only person awake. About an hour into the what-should-have-been-forty-five-minute-trip, I woke up and asked Charon where we were. He had no idea. Turns out, Charon didn't know how to get to Norman. After backtracking a few miles, it took us another hour to finally get to Norman. Yaun-Ti was still passed out cold in the middle of the truck. In fact, he was so passed out that we couldn't wake him. I smacked him around in the face a few times to no avail. Occasionally he'd mumble and then go back to sleep. At one point he told us, "yeah, this is my house" while we were sitting in a grocery store parking lot trying to decide what to do with him (and believe me, dumping him in a shopping cart there in the parking lot had not been ruled out). Finally we decided to simply return back to the party and leave him there. We asked him if that was okay and he responded by leaning over me to vomit out the window. We returned to the party almost four hours after we had left. We carried the scrawny Yaun-Ti into the living room and dumped him on the couch. The next morning, Yaun-Ti said he had no recollection of the night's adventure and found the whole thing rather humorous. He said we should have left him in the shopping cart. I told him I agreed.

There were many, many goofy stories that took place at those two Gatherings. At one point, someone had eaten something bright pink and puked it back up into Ozzy's floor, leaving a bright pink oval on his otherwise tan carpet. Other people had turned Ozzy's spiral staircase into some sort of amusement ride by sliding down the stairs while sitting on cardboard. While all of that was going on, others of us were outside destroying the apartment's parking lot. A couple of guys climbed a stop sign and hung on it until the pole bent in half and snapped off. Others wandered around singing loudly. It was complete and utter chaos. Somehow, our popularity and success online seemed to pervade our real lives.

The day after The Gathering III I returned my father's truck to him. He said that although he didn't really mind the 200 additional miles or the dried puke stuck to the side of it, he was a little curious as to where the stop sign with the pole still attached to it lying in the bed had come from.

During the height of The Brotherhood's reign, I decided the timing was right for me to launch my own BBS. The Gas Chamber, as it was dubbed, would eventually become one of the most popular boards in 405.

The story about the hardware that ran the Gas Chamber is pretty amusing. By 1995, Pentium 60/90/100 processors were being released, while 486 machines were still commonly being used. My main computer at home was a 486 DX4/100, but I didn't want to tie it up running a BBS on it constantly. The machine that would become The Gas Chamber BBS was actually brought into the national computer retail chain I worked at by a customer who wanted us to repair it. The machine was a 386 SX/16, old and somewhat outdated even back then. The bane of our store's existence was people who had purchased three and four year warranties for their home computers. Back then the company's policy was, "if you couldn't fix, it replace it." The morning computer tech could not repair the machine, and as a result the customer ended up taking home a brand new Pentium computer. When I showed up for work that afternoon I found the broken computer sitting on our workbench with a sticky note attached to it that simply read "TRASH." Instead of throwing the machine away I took it home and fixed it. Two dollars and one new battery later, the Gas Chamber was born.

The key to a good warez board was a fast modem and lots of drive space. I already had a top-of-the-line 28.8 baud modem, but the biggest hard drive I had was around 400 meg – not nearly enough to store the kind of warez I intended on trafficking. At that time, new hard drives generally sold for one dollar per meg. The largest hard drive we carried in our store at that time was an 850 meg drive, but rumors began circulating that we would be getting a one-thousand meg drive, which was called a GIGABYTE! Can you imagine? "What on earth would a person *do* with that much drive space?" people asked. I had a pretty good idea. As promised, a few weeks later the new one gig drives arrived with a whopping price tag of $999. Using my employee discount I was able to get the price down to around $700, so that's what I paid.

As time went on I continually spent money on expanding the Gas Chamber. At first the system only had one hard drive, as that was all that old computer case was made to hold. To install a second hard drive I ended up duct taping it to the top of the machine's power supply, as that was the only free space available. I added two more hard drives by removing the computer's internal CD-Rom and floppy drives, freeing up more room inside the machine's tiny case. To compensate for the removed CD-Rom drive I purchased an external six-disc CD-Rom changer that was built like a tank. Each time the drive switched CDs there was an audible KA-CHUNK that would wake me up. It was worth it though; one of my friends had a friend who had limited access to a CD-Rom Burner. At the time, blank CDs cost around ten dollars each. About once a month I'd pull one of the hard drives out of the system and take it over to his house to dump files onto a CD. That way I could still keep the latest games accessible to callers (on CD) while clearing up hard drive space for my uploaders.

From the very beginning, The Gas Chamber was a huge success. The only problem with the board was that it was so busy that people had trouble accessing it. Eventually we added a third phone line to our house, which served as a second incoming line for the BBS and (when it wasn't in use there) served as my "outgoing" data line. And sometimes if both of those lines were tied up I'd stretch the phone cord from the living room into the computer room and dial out on it instead, tying up all three phone lines at once with my computers.

Shortly after it went online, The Gas Chamber became the official World Headquarters of TBH405. In TBH405 Newsletter Issue #11, Yaun-Ti had the following to say about the board:

"There is a system up now known as The Gas Chamber. It will one day, in the weeks/months to come be the best underground system in 405 – possibly even the best 405 has ever had the chance to eyeball. The SysOp? Heh, it's Jack Flack, Mr. I-Net, the man with connections, the shit head with experience, the Flackster. At first glance you will see that it looks like any other system out there (if you even have a chance of getting access since the system will be run by a good friend of mine and a person who can smell lameness a mile away) but that will not be the case. Why? Well let me tell you, asshole. Besides big Jack Flack being the SysOp, he is also the fastest warez trader in 405, and one of the main reasons you little leeches get your grubby hands on 0-day warez. Don't believe me? Well, when (if you ever do) you get access to The Gas Chamber, you will see a huge collection of 0-day shit to gigs of classic files that you kids may have missed. Second, the system will be blessed with affils from across the nation. Third (and like I have mentioned several times in this article already), no lamers stinking up the joint."

One of the biggest secrets behind the scenes of The Gas Chamber (besides the piece of crap hardware it ran on) was its co-sysop. Mr. Moonpie ran the day-to-day duties of the board and performed all the icky administrative duties (like kicking people off the board or griping people out) that I didn't want to do. No one knew Mr. Moonpie's true identity or where he came from.

In reality, Mr. Moonpie was a four-foot tall stuffed toy banana that I picked up from a garage sale for a dollar. As a kid I loved eating banana flavored Moonpie snacks, which is where the overstuffed fruit got his name. So basically, any dirty work that needed to be done on the board I did under this alternate alias. I told Yaun-Ti and The Stranger the story behind Mr. Moonpie fairly early on, but to most other users his true identity remained a secret. As time went on, Mr. Moonpie's history and personality became more developed. One of his trademarks was addressing callers as "ya bastage." Mr. Moonpie developed quite a following over the years and I think many people preferred him to me! In 1995 I got my first digital camera and I slowly began leaking pictures of the real Mr. Moonpie (the large stuffed toy) onto the BBS, letting other users in on the secret. Still, many people still refused to believe that Mr. Moonpie was made up. At The Gathering IV I actually brought Mr. Moonpie along with me, where he was repeatedly pummeled by Yaun-Ti and Prong in a vicious bout of moshing. In 1996 my dog Leroy chewed most of Mr. Moonpie's silk-screened face off including one eye and most of his mouth, but despite injuries the banana lives on. Mr. Moonpie currently adorns the corner of my son's bedroom.

Prong and Yaun-Ti

Mr. Moonpie and Jack Flack during "band practice"
(1995)

Jack Flack and Mr. Moonpie in X-Wing Fighter (1994)

One of the main reasons The Gas Chamber was wildly popular was due to the massive amount of warez I had available for people to download. With all the hard drives and CDs I had added to the system I had tons of drive space available, but it was a full time job keeping it filled with the latest programs for people to download.

I spent an awful lot of my free time downloading software from every board I could find. What I didn't download, my faithful users would upload to me. I taught some of my newer users the "trade" and had them working for me, downloading stuff from other local boards and uploading them to my board. In addition to all this chaos, I had one more source of brand new software that most people didn't have access to.

In the mid-90s, some programs became increasingly difficult to install. Often, complex INI files and other intricate machine settings had to be massaged in DOS to get programs to work correctly – skills most housewives who were simply trying to install games for their children to play did not possess. As a result, it was not uncommon for people to bring their computers into our store to have us install software for them. One day while at work, an opportunity presented itself. A random customer bought a couple of brand new games and dropped off both the games and their computer to have me install them. After the customer walked away from the counter, I made copies of all the diskettes. I then installed the software just like normal on the computer and returned it and the diskettes to the customer when I was complete.

In our tech booth we had a computer with a modem available to us so that we could dial bulletin boards and download drivers or support information. Later that evening when I was the only tech left in the tech booth, I used the computer to call my BBS at home and uploaded the games. I turned off the computer's monitor so that any customers or employees passing by the booth would have no idea what was going on.

From that point on, any time a customer would ask me to install software for them I would make a copy of it for myself, too. If I were working the late shift I would wait and upload the files to my own BBS later that night. If I worked the early or morning shifts, I'd go ask the manager on duty for a box of blank disks and then copy the programs to those same floppies and take them home. If anyone were to ask me what I was doing I would have told them I was making an archival copy just in case I messed up the original floppy, but to be honest I can't ever remember anyone ever asking.

Occasionally, customers would return defective software. More often than not the software wasn't defective but simply wouldn't work with the customer's hardware. Sometimes customers would buy the CD-ROM version of a program instead of the floppy disk version or vice versa. Regardless of the reason, returned software was routed back to the "brown goods warehouse," where it was eventually mailed back to the home office. The brown goods warehouse became my own software hunting grounds. Every day I'd go back and pilfer through the piles of returns, looking for new games. Then it would be business as usual – back to the tech booth to copy and transfer the programs.

After a while I didn't even wait for new programs to make it to the warehouse. I'd simply go out to the sales floor, open whatever I wanted, copy the programs and then go put the box back in brown goods. My continual need for new software outweighed any moral decision-making or rational thinking.

I remember one time a software rep for some company or another showed up asking to see the manager of the computer department. I told him that the manager was at lunch but that I would be glad to help him if I could. The salesman told me he was there to offer us personal copies of a few of their latest programs, so that we (the computer staff) could become more familiar with their products and thus more knowledgeable if customers had questions. I told the salesman that I would gladly hold on to the programs for the manager until he returned. The salesman graciously thanked me for offering to help him and headed on his way. I'll bet he hadn't made it out of the parking lot before I was zipping those programs up and uploading them to every pirate bulletin board in town. Sucker.

Being a member of The Brotherhood of 405 was probably the closest I will ever come to having fraternity brothers. We helped one another, we did favors for one another, and we hung out with one another. In a way it was kind of like high school, except we were the cool kids making the rules this time around. Simply being a member of The Brotherhood could get you access to boards, while being hated by The Brotherhood could get you kicked off just as swiftly. It was like having the ultimate power, which is funny because we gave it to ourselves and somehow got everyone else to buy into the hype.

Chapter Ten
SAZ, SiTH, TDKEB

At the same time I was involved with The Brotherhood, The Stranger and I had started our own group: Soulz at Zero.

During the early 90's, "art groups" experienced an explosion in popularity. Art groups consisted of groups of people who drew pictures on the computer and released them in monthly "packs." Initially art groups released pictures drawn using ANSI or ASCII graphics, while later the art escalated into the world of hi-resolution VGA artwork. The act of sharing one's artwork was not a new idea, as even back in the old days people used to create art and upload it to their favorite local BBSes. What made these different was the packaging style. Similar in design to a legitimate magazine, art packs were released on a monthly basis and usually included a custom viewer, which was essentially a stand alone menu program coded specifically for that group's pack.

The three art groups I followed at that time were iCE, AciD, and TiTAN. In the summer of 1994, TiTAN began including "lits" in their art packs. Lits were poems or short stories members of their group had written. Initially the group's lit section consisted of only a few poems, all of which were really bad.

One day I suggested to The Stranger that he and I should create our own group, a group dedicated to lit. Neither of us had the artistic skills to draw for an art group and wouldn't have wanted to try. However, writing was something we were both interested in. The Stranger was (and is) an avid reader and fan of horror fiction. For him, the group would be an avenue for him to channel his writing energy into. For me, well, I would be the ringmaster – the P.T. Barnum to his juggling act, the Jobs to his Wozniak. "Running my own group" was more important to me than what the group actually was or what it did. With my marketing skills and knack for solving problems combined with The Stranger's writing skills, I knew the group would be a success from its conception. We just had no idea how big it would eventually get.

The formation of just what this group would be was the culmination of many late night walks that took place that summer. I was working nights and living in a run down trailer park at the time. Each night after I got off work, The Stranger would come over and the two of us would walk laps around the trailer park, hashing out the details of our new group. We liked the monthly format that other groups were doing and agreed on that. The Stranger felt strongly that the group should be based around a centralized theme, horror fiction. Although I felt that one theme would get old and be too restrictive, in the end I gave in. If there was any place that would have inspired us to form the world's first horror-based lit group, walking around my trailer park in the middle of the night was it. Ferocious dogs tethered to broken-down cars constantly barked at us, interrupting our conversations. Occasionally a rough looking mutt would appear from out of nowhere and trail us around the neighborhood at a closer-than-comfortable distance.

The last major detail to be decided upon was the group's name. That same summer, a favorite band of mine (Wrathchild America) renamed themselves to Souls at Zero. Somehow I ended up on the band's mailing list, and during that same summer I received a postcard from the band that read, "Some say the body dies, but not the soul, it will rise." For some reason that quote resonated within with me. I also had a Souls at Zero poster, which hung above my computer desk. While kicking around group names, I suggested Souls at Zero to The Stranger. He liked it, although he thought we should change it slightly. As was common among hackers we decided to change the trailing "s" in Souls to a "z", and thus, Soulz at Zero (a.k.a. SAZ) was officially christened.

The first SAZ pack was released on September 13th, 1994. Since every other group released their packs on the first of the month, we had hoped to avoid getting lost in the crowd and draw attention to ourselves by releasing ours later in the month. Plus there was that whole "number 13" thing, being a horror group and all, so we decided to release our packs on the 13th. In the long run all it did was cause confusion, and a few months into the project we began releasing our packs at the first of the month like everybody else.

The debut SAZ pack was, from a design standpoint, atrocious. Knowing what I know now about marketing and brand identities, I definitely should have limited SAZ strictly to literature. One of our early ideas for the group was to make Soulz at Zero packs some kind of multimedia experience for viewers. We wanted to include pictures, and audio, and music, and literature, and package it all up into one big artistic package. Unfortunately without the ability to code a professional (or even presentable) viewer, instead what we released was a mish-mash of random files: lits that had to be viewed with another group's viewer, audio samples of our voices which were pointless and took up too much space, VGA drawings by me that were of poor quality, and a menu system written using the only tools I knew how to use – DOS batch files. While the lits themselves were good, I think the shoddy presentation took a bit away from that fact. Looking back, the early SAZ packs appear very disjointed, disorganized and unfocused to me now.

Public response to the first SAZ pack was lukewarm, but starting up a group always takes a little while to get people's interest and the public's attention. As each successive pack was released, we began acquiring more readers and receiving more attention.

Meeting deadlines was never a problem for The Stranger, a bountiful writer who had a backlog of hundreds of poems and short stories ready to go at a moment's notice. In fact, if I remember correctly he sent me enough poems and short stories over the summer that they became his entries for the first three SAZ packs! And me? I've always been a procrastinator, so I was almost always the weakest link when it came to meeting our self-imposed deadlines. Each month I would keep a small piece of paper on which I would jot down ideas for poems or short stories. On the day before the pack was due to be released, I'd sit down and start writing poems. Once that was done I'd load them into an ANSI editor and add colors and graphics to them. Once that was finished I'd begin the task of cobbling together the huge list of "IF/THEN" and "CHOICE" commands that would eventually become our shabby viewer that month. To this day I'm embarrassed by most of my own work that appeared in SAZ. Had I allowed myself days or weeks to work on submissions instead of hours, I know the quality would have been better.

As the group's popularity began to grow, so did our list of members. Some of those members, like Black Sunshine and Deranged, became members early in the life of the group and remained with us essentially throughout SAZ's two-year span. Unfortunately, many of our other so-called members did not have nearly as impressive track records. Usually mailing us a submission is all it would take to get you listed as a member of the group for a few months. We loved adding people to our member list (to pad our numbers) and hated removing them, which always resulted in people being listed in our "current member" list that we hadn't heard from in months. In fact while going back through the old packs I found at least one person listed in the member list that I couldn't find a single submission from!

Many of our communication issues resulted in the way the group was run and managed, which was completely virtual and online. There were several members of the group who we had never met in person before. In fact, we only knew some of the people simply by their alias. SAZ was formed before Internet access was commonplace, which meant there was no "instant global e-mail" system. We spent a lot of our time leading up to each pack's release date waiting for people to get a hold of us and submit their lits. There was nothing more frustrating than seeing a pack's deadline come and go without hearing from one or more of our members.

One of the most amazing things about Soulz at Zero to me was how it was distributed. Both The Stranger and I ran our own bulletin boards, so when new packs were released they would be put there first. Before long, other bulletin boards wanted to be listed as Soulz at Zero "distro" (distribution) sites, and soon we had half a dozen SAZ distribution sites across the country. After each pack was released, The Stranger would then call all of those long distance boards and upload the new pack to them.

One person whose name will always be tied to Soulz at Zero and who we are eternally grateful for is Faethor. Faethor started out as simply a fan of Soulz at Zero who asked if he could be our official courier. Each month, Faethor would call our BBSes to download the new packs and would then proceed to distribute them to bulletin boards all over the country. He did all of this for no other reason than to simply help us out.

Faethor's phone bill often ran in the hundreds of dollars, but he never asked us for a thing. We always listed him as a member of the group out of appreciation, even though he never contributed any lits to the group. It is generally accepted that SAZ would not have got as big as it did without the time and money Faethor put into distributing our packs.

Another person who eventually took pity on us was Mr. Spock. Another TBH405 member, Mr. Spock eventually coded us a "real" viewer. Even though the most important thing to The Stranger and me was always the literature, our new fancy viewer gave us legitimacy in the scene.

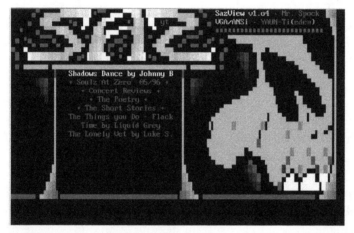

SazView, the Soulz at Zero viewer by Mr. Spock (1995)

Although both The Stranger and I would occasionally get mail from people who had read our packs, it was never enough. As our release count grew, the two of us consistently and publicly complained about the lack of feedback we got from our readers. For many months this turned into a very public love/hate relationship. One month we'd threaten to fold the group since no one was telling us how great we were, and the following month we'd run an editorial claiming we didn't care what anyone thought – Soulz at Zero would live forever!

For the next several months, our little group grew, one pack at a time. Once SAZ really began to take off, we had BBSes across the country begging to be distro sites for us. We were even contacted by readers in other countries! One of the highlights of SAZ for both the Stranger and me was the time we were contacted by a couple of our loyal readers in *Portugal!* To this day we have no idea how our packs made it halfway around the world to someone in Portugal, but somehow they did. For a long time, our fans in Portugal became our battle cry. "Do it for Portugal!" we'd shout and laugh.

As the staff grew, so did our problems. Some months we'd have submissions from ten writers and the next month we might only get things from one or two. And if meeting deadlines was a problem in the early days when there were just two of us in the group, that problem multiplied exponentially once we had a dozen or so contributors. Many packs were released late because we were waiting around for one or two final members to send in their submissions. Sometimes they never came. And unfortunately for everybody involved, neither The Stranger nor myself were particularly good in any sort of management role. Instead, we'd just slam our members in classic passive-aggressive manner publicly in our own packs and hope that they got the message. Some did; others quit.

The Stranger came up with the idea for his own section within Soulz at Zero called "The Death Certificate," which was essentially his own mini-magazine. The Death Certificate contained reviews of horror books and movies, writing tips, horror-related news bits that The Stranger gleaned from magazines and even interviews with other authors. Possibly the crowning achievement of Soulz at Zero was The Stranger's interview with professional horror writer Douglas Clegg. Douglas Clegg actually contacted The Stranger first, to compliment him on his work in The Death Certificate. E-mails were exchanged and eventually The Stranger's interview with Clegg appeared in the pack. We were amazed that people outside the stereotypical modem scene were reading our packs. Over time our packs began including more and more non-fiction articles (like concert reviews and editorials) that got lumped in with the Death Certificate as well.

There are two types of project people: those who don't need feedback and those who do. I'm definitely the type of person who needs it. Every month on the first I'd mail out the newest SAZ pack and then spend the next few hours near the computer, waiting for the kudos and congratulations to come rolling in. They rarely did. After a while, I became convinced that no one was even reading the packs. They were; we know that now in retrospect, but at the time there was no simple way of getting feedback from our readers. Unlike e-mail which is fast and free, to contact us at the time our long distance readers would have had to make a toll call to one of our boards, and people simply wouldn't do that.

I was so sure that no one was even reading our packs that I began to include silly things within them. One of the ones I remember the most was a poem called *Hen House*, which appeared in SAZ pack #8. In the poem, a farmer is killed by a group of murderous chickens that attack him in his hen house. I thought for sure that if anyone were still reading the packs this would get us some feedback, but it didn't.

September 1995 marked the one-year anniversary of Soulz at Zero. By then we were a dozen members strong, and The Stranger and I wanted to put together something really memorable to celebrate the group's first birthday. After spending a couple of nights brainstorming the two of us came up with some neat things to include in the anniversary pack. One thing we wanted to do was include digital pictures of all our members. Digital cameras weren't as common as they are now (this is before camera phones as well), but flatbed scanners were fairly commonplace, so digitizing photos shouldn't have been a big deal. We also came up with an idea in which members of SAZ would write an article about what Soulz at Zero meant to them. We sent out the assignments, sat back, and waited.

The Stranger and I set out to take our own photos for the pack. I didn't have a digital camera yet but I did have a Snappy, a small device that plugged into my computer's parallel port that allowed me to capture stills from videotape. To take our pictures, we used the camcorder my wife and I had received for a wedding present.

The Stranger's orders to me were to take a picture of him that he wasn't in. In other words, he didn't want his face or any other part of him prominently featured in the picture. We knew we wanted something scary to fit the motif, so the two of us drove down to my local cemetery. On the way out the door we grabbed my black trench coat for a costume. While driving around the cemetery we came up with the idea of having The Stranger peek out from behind one of the large headstones. Near the back of the cemetery was a particularly large white stone cross that we decided would work well. So, as inconspicuously as we could possibly do, The Stranger went and posed behind the huge cross in broad daylight while I stood a few feet away from him with a camcorder, recording him. I distinctly remember the groundskeeper circling around the graveyard in his truck, keeping a close eye on the two us who must've looked pretty suspicious.

For the new pack I had written a poem about my image coming out of the mirror to kill someone or another, and I thought a great idea for a picture would be of me climbing out of a mirror. With the tools I had to work with back in 1995, this was easier said than done. While my wife was out shopping one day I pulled her full-length mirror out into the front yard and snapped a couple pictures of it. Then I moved the mirror, posed as though I were flying, and took a couple more pictures. Using cheap software on my computer I merged the two pictures to make it look like I was flying out of the mirror. The background of the picture was filled with mobile homes, so I used the program's paint feature to paint over them with black. Another problem was the grass was filled with all the little poles and hookups that go to people's trailers. To hide them I cut out a picture of the cross The Stranger had been hiding behind in his own picture, shrunk them down real tiny-like and pasted copies of them all over the grass. Like most of my Soulz at Zero art projects the end result did not match the image of what I had hoped for, but it would have to do.

Unfortunately, only one other member of the group (WiSH) submitted anything that month. Most of our plans for the anniversary pack had to be scrapped due to lack of participation. With little new material, the majority of the pack's content was picked from the previous releases and the pack was relabeled a "Best Of" tribute. It wasn't what we had wanted to release at all.

WiSH, SAZ One-Year Anniversary Pack (1995)

Flack, SAZ One-Year Anniversary Pack (1995)

The Stranger, SAZ One-Year Anniversary Pack (1995)

One of my final stunts for Soulz at Zero was the now infamous "dollar bill" poem. A couple of months after the one-year anniversary pack, I put together a generic looking horror poem. The beginning and ending of the poem were normal, but the middle of the poem was a message from me. The message instructed anyone who had read the message to contact me and I would give him or her a dollar. Originally I had wanted to offer five dollars, but I was afraid if word got out about the secret message I'd go broke! So, a dollar it was. Like my other attempts at reaching out to our readers, it failed. In fact, most of our own members didn't even mention to message to me.

The following month, depressed over the fact that seemingly no one was reading the packs any longer, I resigned from the position of co-president of Soulz at Zero. Unfortunately, that didn't mean much. I was still helping The Stranger with the technical aspect of assembling the packs, and after a break that lasted only a month or so, I began submitting articles to SAZ again. Back then I used to attend a lot of concerts, and I was constantly submitting concert reviews that would end up in the Death Certificate. In hindsight they had no business being included in the SAZ packs, but as I once said, "when you found your own group you get to make up the rules too."

The last six months of Soulz at Zero's existence were tumultuous. Outside interest in the group grew inversely to our own members' participation levels. At the height of our popularity, we had to beg for submissions from our staff. It was not uncommon to push back the release date of a SAZ pack for a few days to accommodate late writer submissions. Even though our local support seemed to be dwindling, we were regularly being recognized on a national basis. The Alienist (of Candelabra), Luke Skywalker (of CODiNE) and Mister E. (of Revival/CiA) all submitted literature to our group for publication.

Unfortunately, internal conflicts continued to eat away at the group's core. One of the biggest detriments to the group was how our personal lives had changed. The Stranger had gone from a part-time substitute teacher to working a full time job. Not only had I moved from fast food to the world of government contracting, but I had also gotten married. The two of us simply didn't have the amount of free time to dedicate to the group like we did when it all began. On top of that, the month before the group's two-year anniversary The Stranger and I had a disagreement, which led to us not speaking for a couple of years. For the second anniversary pack The Stranger asked fellow writers from the blossoming lit scene to write a little piece on what Soulz at Zero meant to them. When it was time for the pack to be released not a single person had sent back their comments. That pushed him over the edge. The Stranger assembled the two-year anniversary pack on his own, and officially announced that Soulz at Zero was dead.

Soulz at Zero was the first successful national lit group. I've always considered it a huge compliment that most of our biggest fans were fellow writers. Many lit groups at the time (and some still to this day) cite Soulz at Zero as the reason they began writing or formed their own lit group.

Looking back at the old packs, I'm not particularly proud of what I wrote. Most of the short stories and poems I submitted feel forced. I was never thrilled about being locked into writing horror and I don't think I was particularly good at it. When reading them now, I don't remember most of the submissions attributed to me. Unlike good poetry (which is meant to tell a story or convey a feeling), most of my poems were written out of desperation and a commitment to meet the group's deadlines. I can remember sitting in front of my computer, staring at a blank screen the night before a pack's deadline many times. An idea would pop into my head – guy kills girlfriend out of love, for example – and then I'd bang out a quick poem based on that. Save, clear, next poem. It was not unusual for me to hammer out my three or four monthly submissions in ten minutes or less.

While I'm not necessarily proud of my Soulz at Zero lit, what I am proud of is the group itself. Soulz at Zero at its core was The Stranger and me, two kids from Oklahoma who came up with a wild idea and ran with it. We had no art skills, no fancy programs, no contacts, nothing whatsoever that would have given us an advantage over any other group at the time. What we did have was an original idea, dedication, and passion to make it happen. That's the way I remember Soulz at Zero.

Soulz at Zero showed people that it was pretty simple to create your own group. You didn't need a fancy viewer like the art scene groups had (although it helped) – all you really needed was people who were willing to write. Several of the lit groups that popped up during that time were cheap imitation copies of SAZ. Those didn't last. Many of the ones that did actually show some creativity and originality did gain popularity and found readerships. One such group was 405's own TDKEB.

The five female founders of TDKEB were: **T**ina (Violetta Kitten), **D**ee (Deranged), **K**risten (Black Sunshine), **E**rika (Anacodia) and **B**rittney (Raven). Black Sunshine and Deranged were also members of Soulz at Zero. If SAZ catered to the horror and gothic crowd, the TDKEB girls had every testosterone-filled boy's attention within the area code. TDKEB was more than a lit group – they were a phenomenon. They had their own BBS, which had the boys lining up to call. They also had their own apartment (owned by Black Sunshine and Deranged), where many BBS parties were hosted.

A solid decade before the Spice Girls were marketing "girl power," TDKEB lived it. They took crap from no one. And, they were all girl. Reading their packs was like eavesdropping on your older sister's pajama party. The packs were filled with in-jokes, silly poems and made up rhymes about fellow modemers. They also contained some seriously good lit. There were several short stories and poems that were serious in nature and deserved more public recognition than they got.

At the time the girls all seemed a little scary, dabbling in stuff we were all curious about but too afraid to try. One of my favorite TDKEB stories involves several stories they wrote pertaining to contacting ghosts. A couple of the girls had gotten into contacting ghosts using an Ouija board, and performing so-called "automatic writings" which is supposedly where a spirit writes through the medium by guiding his or her hand. By using the words "so-called" and "supposedly" you can most likely gauge my opinion of the authenticity of this practice. I do have to admit though, the writings the girls were producing seemed pretty realistic, so I decided to try this "automatic writing" out for myself. Years earlier my friend Charon had given me his old Ouija board, made by Parker Brothers and purchased in Wal-Mart. When I went to pull it out of my closet it was missing. I then remembered that I had loaned it to Ozzymandias. After calling Ozzymandias, I got a good chuckle – he had loaned it to the girls from TDKEB! The stories I had been reading involving ghost-writing were being done using *my* Ouija board that originally came from Wal-Mart!

The TDKEB girls were as big of an influence on the local modem scene as TBH was – in fact we often lovingly referred to them as the TBHos. Black Sunshine eventually married Mr. Spock, coder of the Soulz at Zero viewer, and Anacodia dated FalseGod (TBH) for many years before marrying Tekin, another 405 regular.

Small world.

When I resigned from my Soulz at Zero co-presidential duties, I was completely burned out on anything that had anything to do with the group. I was tired of writing horror, tired of compiling the packs, tired of trying to come up with original presentations, and tired of the whole damn lit scene. At that point all I wanted to do was my own project, an e-zine like the old school ASCII ones – no presentation, no fancy graphics, just plain old text files containing articles. Most importantly, I didn't want the hassle of collaborating with anyone else on it. Buster Friendly once told me that all good projects begin with a name. "Pick a good name first," he said, "and the rest of the project will fall into place." Pulling from my Star Wars roots, I decided to name my next project "SiTH" after the evil Star Wars Sith Lords. I then decided SiTH stood for "Sick in The Head." I specifically remember picking the name SiTH first, and then deciding what it stood for second. Once I had a name, I began writing.

SiTH was everything SAZ was not. SAZ was structured, colorful, and had both a theme and a set release schedule. SiTH was simply a collection of text files I had written, combined with a few submissions from other friends. It was crazy and chaotic. And, it was a lot of fun to write. The debut issue of SiTH featured articles like "Drive Thru Blues," "Top 10 Games to Play With a Cat," and "People I Hate This Month." The Stranger also contributed a few entertaining articles such as "Why You Should Kill Yourself" and "Bombing Canada". One article I regret writing and releasing to this day was titled, "How To Have Fun In [Store Name Removed]". In that article I suggested several ways to make employees' lives of said electronics chain miserable. I also described in detail three different ways to shoplift from the same store. The methods I described were simply ways we had discovered people were successfully shoplifting from the store I worked at. In retrospect it was pretty irresponsible information to share, and I've always regretted releasing it.

Fortunately, most of the other articles released through SiTH were simply light-hearted social commentaries, written by me and inspired by the world around me. I wrote articles about people driving on ice, why death penalty executions should be put on Pay-Per-View, and my thoughts on the current state of breakfast cereals.

"Cookie Crisp, now there's an idea for a cereal! The outside of the box now reads, "Bigger and Tastier Cookies!" Well first of all, I don't know what the hell Cookie Crook is thinking. You ever eat one of those things NOT soaked in milk? Let's just say it's not up for any cookie of the year award. Those Keebler Elves don't have anything to fear yet, got me? So now the

cookies are getting bigger. Why don't they just fill the box with freakin'
Oreos? That's a damn cereal idea, 5 Oreos in a box with some milk. And
no prize. Well maybe in the bottom we'll throw in a toothbrush or something
or with 10 box top UPC codes you get a free trip to the dentist. That is, if
you have any teeth left at that point." – SiTH 005

In this day and age, SiTH probably wouldn't have been anything more than a website or a blog, blending in with millions of other websites. Back then, there was no "public online outlet" to release your work, other than Do It Yourself (DIY) methods like e-zines.

One of my favorite SiTH packs is number three, titled "The Best and Worst of 1995." That issue serves as a time capsule as to what was happening both in the real world and the online one. One big news story of 1995 both in Oklahoma and across the country was the bombing of the Alfred P. Murrah building, which I mentioned. On technology, my two "best picks of 1995" were the Internet and the Pentium Processor. By the end of 1995, BBS usage had already begun to wane as more and more people began experiencing the wonder of "the net." Under my "worst of the 1995 BBS scene" section, I wrote the following:

"The bad thing, which seemed to be happening world wide, was the diminishing of the users on local systems. Many good users slowly migrated toward the speed and colors of the Internet, and quit calling locally. Hopefully this is a fad and not a trend …"

Hindsight is 20/20, they say.

SiTH folded after only six issues. Looking back at the packs I can see that there were some hidden gems contained within. One particularly funny piece I wrote was about America's Funniest Home Videos. In it I included rules on how to avoid appearing on the show; for example, don't ever stand anywhere near a piñata. Regardless of how funny some of the articles were, like everything else, it was hard to get people to read the issues, and even harder to get people to provide me feedback about them.

One by one, every local group and project began imploding. Most of them cited "lack of interest" as a common reason, but that lack of interest was stemming from the fact that there was something much more interesting on the horizon, something so huge that it would very quickly extinguish the fire all of us had for our local BBS scene.

More vagabonds: Remission, Light, Yaun-Ti, Buster Friendly (with the peace signs), my wife, and a neighbor who wandered over to see what all the noise was (The Gathering 7)

Chapter Eleven

Hello, Internet!

I remember the day one of my co-workers (Cleric) first described the Internet to me. He defined it as "a large network of servers that you could connect to and get information from." This was back in 1994 (before the World Wide Web had gained popularity), so everything we did was text-only. Cleric eventually gave several of us his account name and password so we could explore this "Internet" for ourselves. Using his local college dial-up account, we had free (and unlimited) access to IRC (Internet Relay Chat) and FTP (File Transfer Protocol). Of course that's all we really needed to start finding trouble.

One of the other TBH405 guys quickly taught me how to retrieve a server's password file. Even though a server's password file could be easily downloaded, the passwords still appeared encrypted. That's what the program John the Ripper was for. Using John the Ripper, we performed both dictionary attacks (trying words from the dictionary as passwords) and brute force attacks (trying every combination of letters and numbers) in order to crack users' passwords. Those cracked accounts could be traded for other working accounts from other Internet Service

Providers (ISPs). Dictionary attacks are quick and don't require much crunching power to perform, but only the simplest of passwords can be quickly revealed. And usually, accounts with simple passwords belonged to students, which had much less access than faculty, staff or admin accounts. If you wanted to crack one of those accounts, it usually had to be brute-forced. By that point in time I had three or four computers in my house, so letting John the Ripper bang away on a password file for a day or two was no big deal. Unfortunately brute forcing a password on one of my slow home computers might take over a week or two, maybe longer. To expedite the process I began cracking passwords on the fastest computers I had access to – servers at work.

Slowly we began to build a collection of administrative accounts, which were highly desirable as they had no "disk quota," or limit to the amount of files you could store on the server. We were now transferring files at record speeds thanks to these new high-speed servers we were using and abusing. At conventional dial-up modem speeds downloading a megabyte of data might have taken 30 minutes or so - now we were transferring that amount in seconds. Of course, those files would still eventually have to be offloaded from those quick college servers to our homes via our slow, wimpy dial-up connections, but that part could be done overnight. Using accounts with a lot of storage, you could acquire tons of new games throughout the day and then connect via your dial account to transfer them back to your house all night long.

Eventually through reading articles and talking to people we began learning simple methods of covering our tracks, most of which involved either erasing log files or hopping and bouncing through multiple connections in order to hide our point of origin. In all honesty, most of what we did to cover our tracks was wasted effort. The fact of the matter was no one really cared what we were doing. Within a couple of months I had admin accounts and the password files from at least ten different local ISPs and colleges, and not a single one had noticed – or if they did, they didn't care enough to try and lock us out or hide their password files. Sure, we weren't doing anything harmful other than using bandwidth taking up huge amounts of disk space, but you would still think our abuse would become obvious at some point. Even the most cursory review of a server's logs should have revealed our activities to any network admin, but times were different back then. The administrators either didn't seem to know or care that we were there or what we were up to.

The biggest advantage hackers had during that time was the incredible rate of speed that technology was developing. Few server administrators could keep up, and even fewer tried. Many so-called "administrators" were either students, volunteers, or employees appointed to the position simply because they were the most computer-literate person in the office. It was never really a fair fight, considering that once these networks were connected to the Internet they were being targeted by the entire world.

The other disadvantage most network administrators had was that hackers began using the Internet to get organized. In hacking-related chat rooms, questions could be asked and answered at the speed of light on a global basis, much quicker than administrators could plug the holes.

During the mid-90s, the motives behind hacking began to change. Prior to the arrival of the Internet "hacking" had always been synonymous with "exploring." And even when we began hacking around on the Internet, the main reason we did so was just to get free Internet access so we could continue to download games and pump them back into our own local BBS scene. At least in the beginning, none of us were hacking just for the sake of hacking. In the beginning none of us thought that the Internet would replace our own local bulletin boards. At best we saw it as something "equal but different" – if nothing else it was a good steady source of incoming warez. As the popularity of the Internet and later the Web began to grow, people started associating "hacking" with "power." And maybe it was always that way, but as the Internet's visibility grew so did the power. If you had multiple shell accounts on multiple servers, you had power. If you had unlimited disk space on a server, you had power. If you could run an IRC bot, you had power. All this power could be used in leveraging online deals for software, or other accounts elsewhere, or access into seedy online back alleys. It gave you a hand up in online bargaining.

Finding warez on the Internet was a simple task thanks to FTP and IRC. IRC is a huge conglomeration of chat channels, many of which were set up for the sole purpose of trading software. Sometimes people would publicly announce in a channel what programs they were offering, and by simply typing a command their computer would send the program to your computer. Other traders were more secretive, lurking in the shadows and demanding goods in exchange for their warez. Goods often equated to other warez, but credit cards, network accounts and FTP sites were also often valid currency.

FTP sites were a lot less hassle than chat rooms and a lot more anonymous. Using FTP, pirates would stash their virtual booty into Internet directories that other users could then connect to and download. Some FTP sites were run just like bulletin boards: users had login accounts, passwords, and most importantly file ratios (which kept users from continually downloading and never uploading) in place. Other FTP sites were simply anonymous dumping grounds. Often these were commercial or businesses' FTP servers that had been compromised. Someone might announce in IRC, "500 meg of warez in ftp.microsoft.com/hacked/pub/warez" which would be followed by hundreds if not thousands of greedy little bottom feeders hammering the FTP site, downloading everything they could get their hands on before either the files were detected by administrators and deleted or the massive onslaught of bandwidth temporarily blasted the site offline.

When my FTP sites would run dry, I'd hang out on IRC for hours at a time, looking for warez to download. One of the best sources for warez on IRC was from the cracking groups themselves. Back then, most cracking groups ran their own public IRC channels where their latest official releases were continually being offered. One day while out trolling for the latest software I joined #razor, home of the infamous cracking group Razor 1911. After joining the channel I received a private message from Maverick, one of the group's members. Maverick recognized the "405" in my handle and asked me if I was in the Oklahoma City area. When I told him I was, he asked me if I would be interested in a position as a courier for Razor 1911. I gladly accepted the position. He then explained to me that my job would be to download Razor programs the minute they were released and upload them to Street Spydrs, his BBS (which just happened to be located in 405).

Let me take a moment to explain (in the simplest of terms) how the online world of piracy works. Cracking groups "crack" software (by removing the program's copy protection) and then give it away for free. That's it. There's no big conspiracy, no ties to the mafia, nobody making any money – that's it. That's not to say that some kid somewhere isn't burning these programs onto CDs and selling them to his classmates, but in general nobody's making a dime off of any of this.

Groups still had positions just like the old BBS days. They still needed people to supply the software to crack, crackers to remove the copy protection, coders to write intros or installers, and of course couriers, to move the files around from place to place.

But now, there were different types of couriers: those who uploaded the group's releases to various FTP sites, those who spread them via IRC, and at least back then, those who were responsible for getting the files onto the group's BBSes. Being a BBS courier was the least desirable courier position as it involved moving large amounts of files over slow phone lines instead of fast Internet connections. For example, I remember the first game I was supposed to spread took up eight floppy disks. To move those eight disks from one FTP site to another took about two minutes. But downloading those disks to my house took over two hours – and then I had to turn around and reupload them to the Razor BBS, which took another two hours. This process was repeated every day. Sometimes multiple games would be released in a single day. And eight disks is just an example. As time went on games became larger. I can remember spreading releases that would take seven or eight hours to download and another seven or eight hours to reupload. More and more often I was tying up all three phone lines with my computers. At night one line would remain connected to my own board while I would be downloading games with the second and uploading warez to Street Spydrs with the third.

And so, once I had been officially hired, downloading and uploading files is how I spent much of my free time. And remember that when I say "hired," I mean "working for free." There are really only two benefits to being a courier and pay is not one of them. The first benefit is the prestige that comes from being associated with a major cracking group. The other benefit is the access to unbelievable amounts of software the minute it is cracked and released. This worked out great for me. As I would download the Razor releases I would store them on the hard drive of my BBS computer first, and then begin to upload them to Street Spydrs, Razor's World Headquarters. In reality this meant that The Gas Chamber was getting Razor releases quicker than their own headquarters! This did not go unnoticed by other 405 locals, who hounded my BBS day and night, constantly downloading new games.

The relationship between Razor 1911 and myself was flaky at best. On the Internet I couldn't get anyone within the #razor IRC channel to even acknowledge me, and the vast majority of messages I sent to Maverick through Street Spydrs were never answered. Occasionally I'd drop him a message inquiring on how I was doing or how things were going, never to hear back. In retrospect I realize now that I was never really a member of Razor to him. I was simply a kid who was willing to tie up tons of his own time and disk space to move some dumb games around in cyberspace. At the time though, it all seemed worth it.

For almost six months I spent time every day checking the Razor FTP sites and uploading new files to Street Spydrs. And then, over a short matter of weeks for reasons I'm not really sure of, the relationship began to unravel. As anti-climactic as is might sound, I'm still not really sure what happened. One by one I began losing access to Razor's FTP sites. Since I was less than nobody in Razor's world, getting information as to what was going on internally within the group was impossible. My messages to Maverick continued to go unanswered. When I would ask what was going on in the IRC channel, people would take turns calling me "LOSER" and "NARC". With any large underground group there's always a certain amount of healthy paranoia (as well there probably should be), but Razor 1911 (at least at my level of involvement) appeared to be little more than disorganized chaos. Over the next few weeks all my Razor FTP sites had quit working and I had nothing to upload to Maverick's board. One time I did actually hear back from Maverick and he told me to not worry about the FTP sites and to just "get the releases from IRC like everybody else." Well hell, I could do that and not even upload them to Street Spydrs, so that's what I began to do. A few weeks later I found my Street Spydrs account had been disabled, and shortly after that Maverick's BBS quit answering all together. There were rumors that Maverick had been busted by "the man," but the board reappeared soon afterward in Houston. Apparently he just relocated.

And with that, my career as a courier for Razor 1911 was officially over.

One thing that cannot be denied is the affect that Street Spydrs had on our local scene. As mentioned, through the efforts of myself and a few others, the level of new software being pumping into our local scene skyrocketed. But more than that, the clout that a group such as Razor brought to our area code was noticeable. It gave 405 credibility.

Razor or no Razor, life went on in 405. The Brotherhood was still trying to hold the scene together, and several of us continued to chat and hang out together in real life. The person I probably hung out the most with during that time was Ozzymandias, the host of Gatherings 2 and 3 and the most insane person I've ever hung around with, which again I mean most endearingly.

Ozzy's claim to fame came in the form of Vinculum Data System (VDS), a local BBS run by a guy named Peter Dimas. VDS was the first multi-line BBS any of us had ever experienced, and as such it was amazing. Prior to IRC and the Internet, online chatting was done one-on-one and usually involved a caller chatting with a BBS SysOp. On VDS, ten or twelve users could get online and chat with one another. While now it doesn't sound very impressive, in 1995 it was mind-blowing.

From the beginning, TBH405 had a love/hate relationship with VDS and Peter. Prior to VDS Peter had run a warez-type board, so some of the brotherhood members saw him as a sellout (not enough to not call his new system, mind you). VDS had a staff of moderators who could squelch (mute) mouthy users, and boot them offline or even ban them if problems continued. One TBH member or another was always getting the boot, which would cause other members to launch some sort of silly retaliation.

VDS started out free, but quickly moved to a pay-for-credit BBS system. Users could send in checks or use their credit cards to buy credits, which translated into online time. There were also ways online to win credits (trivia games, etc) that were popular. On top of all that, you could donate credits to other people, so if someone "popular" was online and was running low, people could donate credits to them to keep them online a little longer. Eventually VDS added another way to purchase credits by adding a 1-900 voice line that people could call. After calling the automated line, users would enter their VDS User ID, credits would be assigned to their account, and the money would be charged to their phone bill.

Or, you know, anyone's phone you happened to be calling from.

One night, several of the brotherhood members were hanging out on VDS and chatting when Ozzymandias logged on. Moments later I got a private message which read, "Ozzymandias has just donated you 1,000 credits." While I don't remember for sure, I seem to recall that one credit equaled one hour of online time, which equaled one dollar. Essentially, Ozzy had just given me $1,000 worth of credits. Soon, other online users began sending each other messages. "Did Ozzy just give you a bunch of credits?" In just a few minutes time, Ozzy handed out over $10,000 in online credits.

I tried to call Ozzy's pager to find out what was going on, but he wasn't home. He was next door, standing outside a no-name Chinese Laundromat, using his phone and alligator clips to call the VDS 1-900 number from the Laundromat's phone line.

It didn't take long for the administrators of VDS to figure out what was going on. I believe the exact message I received was, "Your account has been suspended, prepare for a call from the authorities."

CLICK.

Nothing gets a hacker to clean his room more quickly or more thoroughly than the threat of a visit from the authorities. Within minutes I had yanked computers from their resting positions and loaded them into the trunk of my car. My first thought was to put some rocks in them and toss them into the local lake, although common sense quickly took over and I figured my parents' attic would be safe enough.

Before leaving, I looked up Peter Dimas' phone number in the phone book. I tried the number and after a few rings, Pete answered. Dimas assured me that he wasn't really calling the authorities, but that everyone who had been passing around credits that night was banned from VDS. I told him I understood and that I'd relay the information to the rest of The Brotherhood.

Within a few weeks we all had accounts on VDS again under fake names, but we learned our lesson and kept a bit lower profile the second time around. In a funny related story, a few months later VDS announced they were having a midnight meeting at IHOP and that all their users were invited. I thought it would be a funny idea if Ozzy and I attended the meeting incognito, and so we did.

Ozzy picked me up in his car, the Hearse with no Reverse (which was funny both because it was true and it rhymed). Parking the Hearse with no Reverse took quite a bit of planning; since the car had no reverse gear, any backing up required the two of us to physically push the car backwards from the front grill. After circling the parking lot a few times, we found a suitable parking spot and entered it.

We found the staff of VDS and a few users sitting in a large corner booth in the back corner of the restaurant. (Although we had never met, it is not difficult to spot fellow nerds in public places.) When they asked us who we were, we just made up aliases. Over the next couple of hours, we sat anonymously next to the people that had threatened to send us to jail, talking about computers and bulletin boards while eating pancakes.

Flack, Yaun-Ti, and Prong (Date Unknown)

The Gathering 4 took place during the summer of 1995 and was thrown by my wife and me. The two of us were living in a trailer park at the time and had free access to the park's clubhouse, so we held the party there. While it may sound like a bad idea to invite 50 or so hackers and other socially inept beings to a rented room I would be financially responsible for, it sounded like an even worse idea to invite them to my house all at once. My wife agreed.

Pretty much everybody who was anybody in the local modem scene attended TG4. Josh and Dave (friends of mine) brought a server, hub and network cables and had an eight-machine network up and running for people to play networked games on. In one corner of the room I had a VCR and television hooked up and was showing random movies. In another area I had both my old Commodore 64 and my old Atari 2600 hooked up for people to play. I drug my home stereo along with my huge living room speakers up to the clubhouse along with a couple hundred CDs for music. I also bought a keg of beer and enough hot dogs for everyone invited to have several.

Never underestimate how many people can get really, really drunk off a single keg of beer.

It did not take long at all before things were out of control. Just a few minutes after tapping the keg, people were chasing each around the clubhouse playing tag. Drinks were being spilled and things were being broken. I saw people coming out of the kitchen with hot dog wieners hanging out of their pants. Susan saw other kids just taking the hot dogs I had purchased, breaking them in half and throwing them away for no reason. At one point I looked out the large sliding glass door to see Prong and Digital Anarchist, sitting in the club's hot tub, fully clothed.

When things get out of control I get very stressed out. I can remember walking from person to person saying "please don't do that" over and over. And yet the madness continued for several hours.

I had brought to the party with me Mr. Moonpie – the large, stuffed banana who had been masquerading as the co-sysop of The Gas Chamber. Near the end of the party, two very inebriated TBH405 members Prong and Yaun-Ti decided to start slam dancing with the banana. With Suicidal Tendencies cranking out of the stereo and terrified onlookers gawking, the two of them proceeded to toss poor Mr. Moonpie back and forth, drop him on the floor, and perform flying body slams on him repeatedly – sometimes leaping from the ground, other times launching themselves from off the furniture. The entire time, Yaun-Ti – often with his pants down, screamed "I'M NOT CRAZY" along with the music (despite his actions). I am sure the two of them had multiple bruises the following morning. Mr. Moonpie, for all the wear, suffered only slight stuffing loss.

Things were not always friendly within the modem world. One person who I clashed regularly with was a punk kid named Barry who went by Digital Anarchist. Barry was always reinventing himself under new aliases like Trash Can Man or other goofy names, but once people figured out his ruse they would just say, "oh that's just Barry again."

More than me not liking Digital Anarchist, I think I simply didn't like the new generation of modemers, the epitome of which was him. They didn't trade for warez like we once had; they demanded them. They weren't respectful at people's parties; they were louder, ruder and wilder. When I drank I wanted to laugh and have a good time. These guys wanted to tear stuff up or set things on fire. They just weren't my crowd, I didn't like them, and Digital Anarchist was their leader.

One time, someone sent an anonymous message to Digital Anarchist via his BBS stating that they were turning him in to the FBI for something or other. Digital Anarchist immediately called me, accused me of sending the message, and threatened to call the FBI on me regarding warez. This was not a solitary incident. Whenever you kicked Digital Anarchist off your board, he would call you and threaten to turn you into the FBI. One time I dropped his download credits to zero and he called, threatening to turn me into the FBI. You would have thought the guy had a personal contact at the FBI sitting around waiting to bust people.

I can't remember how or why Digital Anarchist showed up to The Gathering 4 but he did and I somehow put up with him. I remember he left the party earlier than almost everyone else.

After cleaning up the mess from The Gathering 4 I went home to check The Gas Chamber to see what people had posted about the party, but was surprised to find no one had even posted about it. After doing some more investigating I found no one had even called the BBS since the party had begun. I picked up the phone and discovered that there was no dial tone. Behind out mobile home was the phone pedestal. I took the phone and some cable out there to test the jack – it worked fine. When I turned around, I immediately saw the problem. The phone lines running from the pedestal to the house had been neatly cut.

Was it Digital Anarchist? I don't know. I have my suspicions, but no hard evidence. In his defense, to this day he vehemently denies doing it. Maybe it was just a case of being in the wrong place at the wrong time, but the circumstances certainly pointed a finger in his general direction at the time.

Events like these pushed me away from the scene. I didn't want to get into fights or deal with perpetually persecuted kids (or the FBI, for that matter). All I wanted to do was hang out with people online, chat about the good old days, and play games.

One of my favorite things to do was grab a bunch of new games and then take them over to either Charon's or Arcane's house and try them out. For a while PC-based pinball games became very popular. There was one called Pinball Illusions that Arcane and I both enjoyed immensely.

One time, while visiting his house, Arcane challenged me to a pinball duel. Challenge accepted! Susan (my wife) had gone with me as well, so while Arcane and I played pinball on the computer she sat in the living room watching television.

Our average score on the game was around 50 million points, give or take a few. We each took turns, trying to one-up each other's high scores.

Suddenly during one of my games, I hit some sort of crazy bonus and the game started going berserk! I was getting a million points every time the ball hit a bumper! Thwack-thwack-thwack – three million! Bounce-bounce-bounce – another three million! My score skyrocketed. 50 million, 60 million, 70 million! We couldn't believe it! Both of us were screaming at the tops of our lungs and laughing uncontrollably! This went on for a solid minute or two.

All of a sudden, I started getting extremely light headed from laughing and screaming so much! Arcane tried to grab the keyboard and save my game but I thought he was trying to sabotage my record-setting game and I fought him off. I was laughing and hyperventilating so hard that I began to pass out! I started getting tunnel vision and fell out of Arcane's computer chair on to the floor. By this time Susan had come into the room to see what in the world the two of us were so vigorously laughing about. Even lying on the ground I managed to rack up a total of somewhere around 300 million points, the highest score we ever scored on that stupid pinball game.

And while Arcane could give me a run for my money in most games, Charon could not. In all the years Charon and I played games together, there was only one I remember him consistently beating me at: Top Gun. In this stupid game, you and a friend dog fight and try to shoot each other out of the sky. Charon would shoot me down in record time, every single time.

Every gaming session with Charon would begin with a bunch of new games, every one of which I would slaughter him in. Game after game I would destroy him, hands down. And then, he would ask the inevitable question.

"So, you wanna play Top Gun?"

So, we would play and he would mercilessly fill my ship with hot lead, sending me careening down through the clouds and crashing into the ground below. You would not believe the hours I spent practicing that damn game in hopes that I would win just *one* match during *one* set during *one* game we played, but I don't think I ever did.

I seriously, seriously hated that game.

All I really have are fond memories of those days. I spent my days downloading games, uploading games, and playing games. I talked to my friends constantly either online or over the phone, and I worked in a computer department. Life was good.

While the Internet was fun and useful, it wasn't very accessible to the average computer owner – and we kind of liked it that way. If it had been left up to us geeks, I'm not sure the World Wide Web would have ever been invented. But it was, and before long millions of people would begin flooding into our own personal electronic playground.

Chapter Twelve

The Downward Spiral

I clearly remember the first time I saw World Wide Web. It was in the spring of 1995. While chatting on the telephone with my old buddy Arcane, he began telling me about how great he thought the Internet was. I agreed with him. Boy, downloading files, sending e-mail, using IRC and FTP – man, wasn't it great? But then he corrected me and explained that he was talking about something called the World Wide Web, and I remember having absolutely no idea what on earth he was talking about. He went on and on, talking about this new Internet thing with pictures, and sound, and colors. Was the man delirious? I decided I was going to have to check out this new so called "graphical" Internet stuff for myself, so off to Arcane's I went.

When I got to Arcane's apartment and saw the web for the very first time, I was completely blown away. I can still vividly remember the Star Wars website he first showed me. The Star Wars logo sat at the top of the page, pictures of lightsabers served as horizontal page dividers, and a MIDI version of the movie's classic theme played over and over in the background.

While Arcane was showing me how hyperlinks worked and the basics of HTML, I can remember thinking to myself over and over, "oh my God." I remember thinking that this was going to be huge among the computer savvy crowd, but I had no idea how commercial and public it would all become someday.

When I buy a new car, I never sell my old car first. I'm always afraid that I'm not going to like the new car as much as I liked my old car, so I always hang on to the old car until I'm sure I like the new one better. And while the new car with it's fresh new car smell always eventually wins me over, letting go of an old vehicle is always a slow process for me.

For a long time, the Internet scene and the BBS scene were two separate worlds. The BBS scene was *our* scene. It's where my friends hung out. It was close and comfortable. It was familiar, and it was my home. The Internet seemed different: foreign and cold. It was a good source of software, but it wasn't a good place to make friends. I never considered the thought of the Internet killing the BBS scene as to us they were two completely separate experiences. In the BBS world you had an identity associated with your alias. You had posts. You had a reputation. You had meaningful conversations with your friends. On the Internet, everything was anonymous. There was no connection between a user and a web page. You didn't have to actually know someone to visit their website. That was the piece that was initially missing for me. There were Internet newsgroups, but with the readers we had at the time they were difficult and confusing to use. It wasn't until years later when I saw my first web-based forum that I thought someone had captured the spirit of the BBS message base. The first time I saw a web-based forum, I knew the days of the BBS were numbered.

Soon Internet service providers (ISPs) began differentiating between "Internet access" and "World Wide Web access". One of our local state universities began offering WWW access in early 1995. Fortunately for us, it was also the same university that was known for having horrible password security. Shortly after making the discovery, all of the TBH405 members (along with our friends and our families) now had free web access. This was very valuable, as at the time many ISPs had a maximum amount of time a user could spend online each month, and exceeding that amount of time was quite costly.

As I began to show my co-workers this new world of online information, one of them showed me something new as well. It was a new online service named America Online (AOL), and more importantly, my co-worker said he knew how to access it for free.

Late one afternoon around the end of the business day, my co-worker showed me a neat little program called AOHell. In the beginning, AOL allowed users to apply for free guest accounts that would last for 30 days. Apparently so many people were just using free trial accounts month after month that AOL changed their application process slightly to require a working credit card number with each application. That change kept underage kids from applying and abusing their system. The AOHell program automated AOL's entire application process. It randomly generated names, telephone numbers, and as we soon discovered, credit card numbers. The credit card numbers weren't real of course, but they passed whatever security algorithm AOL was using to check their authenticity. By simply running the program, AOHell would generate you a free AOL account that would last either 30 days or until someone realized the credit card number was fake, whichever came first.

These AOL accounts were worthless for stable e-mail as they frequently died, but they were good for free online access. They were also good for signing up to "warez e-mail lists," which were automated mailing lists that would deliver megs of the latest illegal software to your inbox 24 hours a day. Each day I would log into AOL, check my e-mail, download the programs I wanted from my inbox and delete the next, freeing my mailbox up for the next day's deliveries.

We also discovered how easy it was to get pictures of boobies. There were dozens of IRC channels set up for the sole purpose of delivering naughty pictures of naked women to young men. We used their services frequently and traded the pictures between ourselves like playing cards.

This went on for months at work. My co-workers weren't into hacking or the warez scene but they *were* into games, so I regularly supplied our team with the latest and greatest. Our work area was segregated from the rest of the floor and all of our computers were networked together, allowing us to spend many slow afternoons providing phone technical support while playing multiplayer network games such as Doom II, Descent and Virtual Pool. As much as Windows 3.11 sucked, it did allow for multitasking, which allowed us to flip back and forth between our games and our work screens.

A few months later I was out of the office, away on travel for a week a thousand miles away from home. While I was working at one of our remote locations, I received a phone call. After picking up the phone, I heard a co-worker's voice, whispering franticly into the phone.

"They found it," he whispered.

"Found what?" I asked.

"Everything," he replied. "The games, the pictures, the AOHell stuff. Everything. They're scanning all the computers right now. They scanned yours first."

My heart sunk. Instantly I felt like I needed to throw up. I knew I was going to be fired; that was a given. What I didn't know was just how much trouble I was going to be in. Were they going to press charges? Where they going to sue me? My mind was racing. Suddenly, using a program that generates fake credit card numbers, stealing Internet access and cracking password files while on computers at work didn't seem like such a good idea.

For the rest of the day I waited for the phone call letting me know I'd been fired, but it never came. I worked the entire next day with butterflies in my stomach like I was waiting to be called into the principal's office. But I never received the call. Had they missed it? Had I gotten away with something?

I flew home over the weekend and checked my answering machine. Nothing. Monday morning I showed up to work as usual – although truth be told, I did bring a couple of cardboard boxes in the trunk of my car with me, just in case. When I got to work I found a handwritten note stuck to my monitor that simply read, "Come see me." It was signed by my boss, who also happened to be the meanest woman I'd ever met in my life. Before going to see her I packed my personal belongings into a cardboard box and loaded them into my car. Just in case.

I walked around the corner to my boss' office, ready to take my punishment like a man. She looked up at me from behind her desk, her beady black eyes staring right through me.

"Let's take a walk," she said. I said nothing. When my boss walked past me and down the hall to the elevators, I thought for sure she was escorting me out to the parking lot. At least I'd already packed my stuff – that would make the final few moments a bit less awkward.

Instead of stopping at the ground floor like I'd assumed we would, we went down into the basement to an area I'd never been to before. Maybe they were going to interrogate me or beat me with rubber hoses down here or something. We walked past rows of unlabeled doors to a set of double doors at the end of the hallway. The doors opened up into an old abandoned loading dock. The two of us leaned up against the yellow railing and she lit up a cigarette. Neither of us looked at the other. We both just stared off into space.

"Listen," she said as she took a long drag from her cigarette. "I've got plans for you around here. You got me?"

I nodded.

"They don't involve you screwing up like this. You got me?"

I nodded again, ashamed and embarrassed.

We stood there together, silent, for a few more minutes. Eventually I built up enough courage to speak.

"Are you going to fire me?" I asked.

There was a long pause.

"No," she said. "But I probably should. Now get your ass back to work."

I agree. She probably should have. After my close call, I cooled off for a bit, especially at work. I quit using AOHell and went back to using hacked college accounts that were relatively safe (and untraceable). At work we moved into new cubicles and I picked one far away from everyone else with a great view of oncoming foot traffic. I quit sharing games with co-workers and quit talking about illegal activities at work.

One day at work we got a new toy: our own CD-Rom burner. Through the luck of the gods it was determined the unit would sit on my desk and stay connected to my computer. Blank CDs were still so expensive that each disc we burned at work had to be accounted for, but I gladly bought my own blanks now that I had access to a burner. By now I had accumulated thousands of floppy diskettes. I began bringing boxes of disks to work everyday, and in between calls I'd copy them one by one over to my hard drive. Once I had 650 Meg of programs assembled I would burn a CD, praying the entire time that my computer wouldn't hiccup and ruin a $10 disc. The burner we had was quite finicky and you had to close every other program running on your computer in order to burn discs reliably. Even the sound that announced you had new e-mail could cause the stupid thing to crash. Each finalized disc would be taken home and rotated into my board's CD-Rom Changer. Not that it mattered much by that point. Most of my callers had begun their final migration to the Internet.

The never-ending accumulation of warez had begun to take its toll on me. With calls to my board declining there didn't seem any reason to continue dedicating hours upon hours to building my board's file collections. I began losing interest in the BBS. Of course The Brotherhood was still around at least in name, and with my new found free time I began working on a couple of other projects, like Flack (the album) and Flack (the movie).

Flack (the album) started out as a one-hit joke. One day a funny idea for a break-up song came to me. The song was titled "You Never Told Me You Were A Leper" and was basically four minutes worth of leper jokes that rhymed. *"My first memories of you still linger, I shook your hand and off came your finger."* No real depth, but entertaining (at least to me) nonetheless. After recording a rough version and playing it for The Stranger, he encouraged me to come up with some other songs, and I did. There was "The Ballad of OJ," a song that talked about how sad it was that an innocent man had been accused of murder, "Don't Take My Picture Please," a song from the point of view of a celebrity who doesn't like to have his picture taken, and about ten others. The highlight, according to many people, was "The Ballad of 405." Yaun-Ti penned the lyrics in about an hour and e-mailed them to me one day, hoping I could turn the epic poem into a song. He said he wanted it in the style of Iron Maiden. Unfortunately for him my musical talents and equipment limited me to the style of The Sex Pistols on a bad day. Regardless, I did the best

I could. When released, "The Ballad of 405" would become a staple of 405's history.

Another project I worked on for a while was an untitled movie starring myself, Mr. Moonpie, and another inanimate object, Mr. Codfish. The movie was a series of (very) loosely connected parody sketches. One was a parody of COPS, in which I arrested Mr. Moonpie and roughed him up a bit. The second sketch was a lengthy X-Files parody in which Mr. Moonpie was abducted by aliens. The third skit was a re-enactment of the O.J. Simpson trial, filmed in my refrigerator. O.J. was played by a jug of orange juice, Marsha Clark was renamed Marshmellow Clark and was played by several large marshmallows stuck together, Judge Lance Ito became Ito Burrito and was played by a frozen burrito, and the jury was represented by a dozen eggs with faces on them. Mr. Moonie defended O.J., of course. None of the skits were related in any way, and eventually the project was abandoned due to lack of interest. It's still pretty funny to watch, though, and it gave me something to do to keep my mind off the fact that the BBS world was rapidly dying.

One thing these two projects had in common was that I started them both with very little technical knowledge on how to accomplish them. Someone told me that most albums were recorded on "four-track multitrack recorders," so I went to a local music shop and bought a used one. This of course proceeded the days of affordable software-based multitracking on PCs. All the drum tracks for the album were either created on a $10 drum machine I picked up at a garage sale, or were drum samples I stole from other songs and looped on my computer. *The Ballad of 405* used the drum into from Guns N' Roses' *Rocket Queen*; *Flack* (my theme song) used the drums from the beginning of Devo's *Whip It*. The Mr. Moonpie movie used similar inexpensive techniques, with simple editing performed by hooking two VCRs together and cut scenes made by hand drawing pictures on the computer and putting them into Microsoft PowerPoint. From a technical standpoint both projects weren't very impressive, but they were both fun to do and people enjoyed them. When I look back at them today I think about how much better they both could have been using today's technology. So many ideas, so little time.

I really don't remember making a conscious decision to take The Gas Chamber offline. I just remember noticing one day that people had stopped calling. The Gas Chamber had more drive space and more warez than practically any other accessible system in 405, but I could no longer get people to call. I used to call the board every day from work to ensure it was still running, and near the end it got to the point where that call might have been the only one the board got each day. In the spring of 1996 my wife and I moved out of the trailer park and into a real home. At that same time we dropped the third phone line, and I never bothered to put the board back online in our new house. Like so many other boards, The Gas Chamber went away not with a bang but with a whimper. I pulled the plug, and in an instant my years of hard work vanished from existence. There were few people left in the modem scene who cared.

The Gas Chamber was one of the last big local boards I remember being online. Shortly after it went offline, the Brotherhood of 405 was officially unofficially dissolved. Former members gravitated to IRC and claimed #405 on efnet, where they (and occasionally I) still hang out today. A few of us ran small private FTP sites and shared software and music between us, but eventually those went away too. It became difficult to keep track of one another through the Internet. Some people moved on, other people still hang out. The death of the BBS was the death of the local scene. If the Internet was the sound of a gun hammer being pulled back, the World Wide Web was the explosion of a bullet blowing it to pieces, putting a wounded beast to rest.

In the fall of 1996 I accepted a job position in Spokane, Washington. The Gathering 5 was held a weekend or two before Susan and I moved across country. The Gathering Five had a different vibe than the Gatherings before it. Wamprat, a friend of Buster Friendly's, hosted the party. The age gap was immediately noticeable; Wamprat was the same age as my parents while most of the party attendees weren't old enough to legally buy their own beer. Most of the people who came were younger than me and they represented the new generation of "computer kids" – kids who were growing up on the Internet. Some of the kids at the Gathering weren't even familiar with the local scene and had only found out about 405 through the Internet. The Gathering 5 was tame by Brotherhood standards, although I did debut the Flack album at the party and sold copies for five bucks a tape. It was an anticlimactic going away party.

I left for Spokane a month before my wife did. While she stayed behind in Oklahoma to sell our old house and tie up loose ends, I was to drive 1,800 miles across the country to set up our new living quarters.

Planning has never really been my thing. For the trip I packed my car with the essentials: every music CD I owned, a 13" television, a couple of computers and a duffel bag full of clothes. I only forgot a few, small items: a toothbrush, a pillow, a blanket, dining utensils, deodorant, etc. Most of those items were picked up at Target shortly after I arrived into town.

My first day in Spokane, I was completely lost. After wandering around town a bit I found some mobile homes that were available for rent a week at a time. The one I ended up in was divided into two sections. A family permanently lived in the front half. I got the back half, which consisted of one bedroom and a bathroom. My next-door neighbor for the week was a crazy hippie chick who lived in a school bus with a tie-died Jimi Hendrix tapestry hanging down over the windshield. One night she knocked on my door and asked if she could use the phone. I said sure, and let her in. She stayed on the phone for almost two hours, calling one friend after another. I finally told her she needed to wrap the calls up because I was getting hungry and wanted to go get some dinner. I think she even talked me into picking her up a couple of burgers, too. I spent the rest of the week trying to avoid her.

The worst part was, I felt so unsafe at the place that I was too afraid to leave my stuff in my car. Whenever I would get to the trailer I would unpack all the computers, CDs and everything else into the trailer – then, when I would leave to go pick up lunch or dinner, I would load it all back into my car because I was too afraid to leave it there either!

A few days later I found a nice apartment that was available, so I said goodbye to my kooky bus-living neighbor and moved into the apartment. I picked up a foam floppy chair from Target that converted between an uncomfortable bed and an uncomfortable chair, and that's the only furniture I owned until Susan arrived with the rest of our stuff. I sat the chair up against a wall and arranged my CD player, my computer and my television around me in a semi-circle. It was a bachelor's dream pad.

.

The first month or two I was in Spokane I picked up a couple of local computer magazines, the kind that always had local BBS numbers listed in the back of them. Unfortunately, the Washington BBS scene was drying up, just like the Oklahoma scene, just like everywhere else.

Once I had a phone line I called the first local Internet provider I could find, and set up an account. I spent a lot of my time in Spokane learning about the web, specifically HTML (the most basic language used for coding web pages). Through the web I was able to e-mail my friends and family back home. I also chatted regularly with my old BBS pals through IRC.

One IRC channel I frequently visited was called #oldwarez. Essentially the channel was filled with people just like me, people who loved the old days of computers and loved talking about older games. Talk about finding your niche. Without much of a social life otherwise, I would sit on the Internet for many hours at a time, talking about the old days to both old friends and new.

One of the guys in #oldwarez I became friends with was a channel operator ("op") who went by Gestap0. Gestap0 and I had a ton in common including our love of old games and old computers. Gestap0 lived in Edmonton, Canada (a good 12 hour drive from Spokane), but with little else to do, I agreed to drive up to Edmonton over a weekend and hang out with him.

I'd never been to Canada before, so the trip to Edmonton was both interesting and exciting. When I crossed the border into Canada, the border patrol asked me if I had anything to declare.

"Like what?" I asked.

"Fruit, alcohol, tobacco," they said.

"Nope, none of those!" I happily replied. I had at least three complete computer systems, several boxes of pirated CDs, my PlayStation and a bunch of other electronics, but no fruit, alcohol or tobacco! They smiled, I smiled, and off I went into the Great White North.

I spent the weekend hanging out with Gestap0. He showed me how to load Linux on a box. We played games and traded games. Gestap0 took me to visit the West Edmonton Mall, the largest mall in

North America. It was unbelievably large. He also took me to Taco Bell, where I was shocked when I ordered two tacos and they asked me if I wanted fries with that. I told them I had never heard of such a thing in the U.S.

"What do you have with your tacos then?" they asked.

I shrugged. "More tacos, I guess," I replied.

I got a later start home than I had planned, and I arrived at border crossing sometime Sunday night around midnight. The guard at the border, noticing the large amount of computer equipment I had packed in my car, asked me for my paperwork.

"What paperwork?" I asked.

The guard asked me where all the computer equipment had come from and I told him I had taken it on a visit to see a friend in Edmonton.

"Sure you did, eh," he said.

(I don't really think he said the stereotypical Canadian "eh", but I always throw that in when I retell the story. So here it is for you, as well.)

I never did figure out exactly what they thought I was doing, but before long I found myself sitting in a border crossing building with a guard standing near me as other employees first emptied my car and then began meticulously searching it. The hood, trunk, and all four doors of my poor Dodge Neon were wide open as Mounties emptied everything I had taken on my trip with me out in the parking lot.

My biggest concern were my CDs, which were labeled with such inconspicuous names as "WAREZ 14" and "XXX 7," but my secondary concern were the three monitors which belonged to the government and had very large government barcodes stuck to them (I had borrowed them for my weekend voyage).

This went on for a couple of hours, not because they were finding anything but because I don't think they knew what to do with me. A couple of times the guy in charge came in and asked me the same questions – who I was, where I had been, where I was going, what the hell all that stuff in my car was, and why hadn't I declared it.

"Because," I repeated, "it wasn't fruit, alcohol or tobacco."

At the two-hour mark, I decided it was now or never. When the head guy came back in, I asked him if I could use their phone. When he asked me whom I was going to call, I told him my boss.

"Look," I told him. "If I'm not at work by 6AM, some very important government systems won't come online, and some very high up government officials are going to be pretty pissed off."

Now, let's get real for a second. Yes, I worked for the government – as a flunky computer specialist. If I didn't show up for work the following morning, it would mean exactly squat. Heck, my work might not have even noticed me missing for a day or two.

Whether they bought my story or just plain felt sorry for me, shortly after my stand they began loading all my things back into my car and sent me on my way. The guy in charge gave me a stack of paperwork to fill out and told me I needed to file taxes or claims or something or other on all the stuff I had brought with me across the border. I swore to him I would and, shaky and sweaty, got back into my car to finish the last leg of my trip.

The paperwork went right out the window on US-95, somewhere between the border and Spokane. Jack Flack always escapes.

Susan and I lasted eighteen months in Spokane. By then we were more homesick than we had ever been. Though some networking we found jobs back in Oklahoma, and soon we were back on the road, heading home.

By the spring of 1998, the modem scene was completely gone – migration to the Internet was complete. At least the channel #405 helped us feel as though there was some sense of local community, but before long people from other area codes began hanging out in our channel, and likewise, many of the local users quit dropping by. At any given time you can still find half a dozen or so old modemers still hanging out in the channel, but it's a far cry from the strong numbers we once had.

The last time most of the TBH405 members were in the same room was, I suppose fittingly, at a funeral. In the spring of 2002 I received tragic news that former TBH405 member Ghost in the Machine (GitM) had committed suicide. Funeral arrangements were e-mailed between friends and posted on my website along with a map to the funeral home from Mapquest.com and a digital photo of GitM from one of the Gatherings. I suppose it was only fitting that we coordinated our attendance to a former Brotherhood member's funeral completely online.

On Saturday, March 23rd, 2002, a dozen or so former TBH405 members gathered to say goodbye to one of our own. Yaun-Ti, Prong, FalseGod, Violetta Kitten, Gatoperro, Rivas, Anacodia and several others were all there. FalseGod, a personal friend of GitM's, was also a pallbearer. I'm sure there were others I'm forgetting – the whole event still seems like a bad dream to me. I remember being surprised by seeing so many modemers dressed in decent clothes instead of our normal party attire. I hadn't seen most of these people dressed up before; hell, some of them I hadn't seen sober before!

While funerals are never fun, those for young suicide victims are perhaps even more grim. The people standing in the foyer waiting to enter were particularly quiet. Before I took a seat I spent a few minutes looking over a collage some of GitM's friends had put together. The top of the collage had his name written across it and it struck me weird that it read "Scott" and not "Ghost in the Machine." There were a couple of pictures of Scott riding a motorcycle and I remember wondering if I really even knew this kid at all. I didn't know that part of his life, that's for sure. I had stood next to him at a couple of concerts and I'd talked to him online many times over the years, but apparently I didn't know much about his real life. It struck me as being very sad. And I'm sure there were just as many people in attendance that day that had no idea that Scott was a part of our extended online family. I doubt they would ever understand how people who only knew one another from written words on a computer would care enough to attend his funeral.

GitM slaps a sticker on someone's back (TG7, 1998)

While several of the other guys carpooled to the funeral, I drove alone. After the funeral was over I drove out to my thinking spot, a big flat rock located on the northwest side of Lake Overholser where a person can sit and listen to the waves lap at their feet. There are trees, dirt, and other big rocks that you can lean up against, and the way the lake's designed you really can't see anyone else and no one else can see you. It's a great place to go sit and be alone after a funeral. I sat down on those rocks for several hours that afternoon, thinking about the relationships I'd formed with my online friends over the years and wondered if they meant anything at all.

It would be a deceitful and cheap to imply that Ghost in the Machine's death led to the death of the Brotherhood – the modem scene had dissipated years prior, and other than chatting with one another through IRC most of us weren't even hanging out together anymore. Still, the two events remain intertwined in my memory. It was the last time most of us were together in the same room together. With the death of the BBS had come the death of hanging out with your "virtual" friends in real life. Not only had all my old friends grown up, they had grown "out" – finding new friends thanks to the information super highway. Scott's funeral serves as a finite point in time that I can point to and say, "It was over." There would never be another Gathering. There would never be another reunion. The BBSes were gone, and without them, an era had officially ended.

It was over.

Chapter Thirteen

Retroville

I still talk to some of my old modem friends on a regular basis, although we don't do it through BBSes any longer of course. These days we keep up with one another through blogs, sites like MySpace, and of course e-mail. All of those methods are faster and more efficient means of communication than BBSes ever were. In fact from a strictly technical viewpoint, the Internet outperforms vintage bulletin boards in basically every category.

The majority of BBS users chatted, participated in message boards, played online games and traded software. In a head-to-head comparison, the Internet bests bulletin boards in each of these areas. Instead of one-on-one chats between a caller and a sysop, hundreds of thousands of Internet users now chat on IRC. On bulletin boards, conversations often took weeks or months for a thread to unfold; BBS message boards succumbed to online forums and Usenet, where discussions often explode within minutes. Slow, turn-based online strategy games have been replaced by action games that are played in real time by thousands of people. And the exchanging of both legal and illegal files is simpler, easier and much, much faster via the Internet than it ever was on underground bulletin boards. Most games are now merely a search engine away.

So if the Internet is so much better than bulletin boards were, why do so many people miss the BBS era?

There are three major differences I see between then and now. The first is the sense of community that bulletin boards offered. Many of the people I met through bulletin boards became lifelong friends of mine. I still talk to Arcane, FalseGod, and The Stranger once a week, maybe more. Don't get me wrong; I've made a few real life friends through the Internet as well, but the great majority of the people I've met on the net don't live close enough to me to facilitate real life friendships. Sure, there are yearly gatherings, conventions and such where I might meet up with a few of my online friends, but for the most part the friendships I've developed through the Internet tend to stay on the Internet. Bulletin boards were not like this. After meeting Arcane, the two of us spent every weekend together our parents would allow for two years straight, and we remain friends today long after our Commodores have been retired from active duty. Arcane was one of my groomsmen at my wedding (in fact, three of my four groomsmen were Commodore owners), and in 2001 I named my son after him (after his *real* last name – no, my son's name is not Arcane). Those are the kinds of bonds that developed through bulletin boards between modem users. This level of friendship rarely forms between Internet acquaintances.

Arcane with my Son (2001)

Jack Flack and Arcane (Flack's wedding, 1995)

The vast amount of distance between users makes the Internet much more anonymous than bulletin boards ever were. Especially on underground boards, it was in a sysop's best interest to know the true identity of every person who called his board. Every user that called my board had to provide a real name and a voice telephone number, both of which were manually verified before he or she was granted access to my system. Sysops of larger boards often held BBQ cookouts at local parks where users would gather and meet one another. It was one of the advantages to living in close proximity to your visitors, something that's been lost on the Web.

I can remember lying in bed late at night, my eyelids heavy and tired, and hearing *the* noise – the screeching sound of two modems handshaking, one welcoming the other into its domain. You could turn the modem's speaker completely off, but I never did; I always liked knowing when someone was dialing in. The flashing lights from my disk drive would fill my dark room, and my heart would race knowing that somebody somewhere in the middle of the night was sitting at their computer, talking to mine. It's a thrill the Internet cannot come remotely close to duplicating.

Another difference between bulletin boards and the Internet is that the Internet is intertwined with business. Our bulletin boards didn't have pop-up ads or subscription fees. You never saw commercials or billboards mentioning them. Big corporations did not run them. They were owned and operated by fellow computer enthusiasts. There was no financial gain, no hidden agenda behind running a board. They were run for fun for us, by us, so to speak.

The third major difference between then and now was the average user's level of computer competence. As I mentioned in the beginning of this book, early computer systems were expensive and not overly user friendly. Getting just the right Hayes commands to work with your specific model of modem often took trial and error. Adding a second Commodore 64 disk drive to a system required owners to disassemble the brand new drive and scratch off one or more solder traces. Veteran PC users installed their own RAM and hard drives because we had to. Owning a computer was not for the weak of heart, and operating one was a far cry from the simplicity that GUI operating systems such as Windows 95 introduced to the masses. The BBS world was filled with smart, technically adept people, and while many of those same people now access the Internet, it often seems we are now outnumbered.

While writing this book I attempted to contact several of the people mentioned throughout it, with mixed results. At one end of the spectrum I found people like me, people that got into computing and stayed there. Many of my former BBS pals went on to work within the computer industry: FalseGod works for Dell, Dr. Phrackenstein works as a web developer for the state of Oklahoma, and Charon owns his own data warehouse company. On the other end I found people who had all but forgotten the old BBS days. One of the most surprising of which was Klatu, my old partner in crime from the OK Krackers. I hadn't spoken with Klatu in almost fifteen years, and he was quite surprised to receive a call from me. When we spoke he told me that shortly after the two of us had lost contact, he gave away his entire Commodore computer setup including his enormous software collection to a less fortunate family in his church. I couldn't believe it when he told me that he didn't touch a computer for another ten years. I never would have imagined him getting out of the hobby. These days Klatu is heavily involved with Civil War reenactments, only using his computer for checking e-mail and updating his club's website.

Klatu didn't remember most of the people and adventures I mentioned to him during our phone conversation, and he wasn't alone. Several of the people I tracked down admitted to me that to them, the world of BBSes was ancient history. Sometimes the mentioning of a topic or story to them would spark a memory, and sometimes they would spark mine by doing the same. After each conversation I would take my new combined pool of knowledge and contact the next person on the list. Through this method I was able to flesh out many stories that I originally couldn't remember the details of.

I was never able to figure out the reason why some people hung on to those memories more tightly than others. Maybe it had to do with the age of the participants? I'm not sure either of the two groups (those who remember and those who have forgotten) truly understands the other.

Due to my love of the past, for many years I felt like a loner. In 1996 I still had an Atari 2600 hooked up in my living room, almost 20 years past its prime. Don't get me wrong; I like new technology, I just haven't let go of the old stuff yet. In 2002 I discovered a website named Digital Press, which is dedicated to "keeping the classics alive." True to their word, every day the Digital Press forums are filled with conversations about games both new and old. The conversations usually deal more with videogame consoles than with computers, but the people are good people and I found myself visiting the site frequently.

Whenever a message thread about old computers would appear, the same names always jumped into the conversations with me. Icbrkr and Phosphor Dot Fossils (PDF), both Arkansas adoptees, have histories that mirror my own. Both of them were big into their respective local BBS scenes as youngsters. Icbrkr was primarily a Commodore user while PDF actually owned another Franklin Ace 1000. Small world!

The three of us hit it off, and before long, we were visiting one another's houses. Icbrkr and his wife have driven to Oklahoma on several occasions to shop and visit, and I've visited their place as well.

When I make the trek out to his neck of the woods, PDF usually hops over and joins us. Rarely do we have an agenda that involves more than playing old games and talking about the days of yore. And the more I talk with them, the more I realize that my experience growing up wasn't unique. Area codes across the globe experienced the same things: the growth, exploration and eventual demise of the BBS world. Despite the fact that none of us knew each other back then, it is amazing how well we can relate to one another when talking wistfully about "the good old days."

Flack, Icbrkr and PDF in Ice's gameroom (2005)

In the summer of 2004, an Associated Press reporter interviewed me for an article he was writing about the resurgence in retro videogame popularity. My name, comments, and even a photo of me standing next to a dozen or so of my arcade cabinets made their way into the final AP article, which ran in newspapers and on websites across the globe. I got calls from friends and family alike telling me they had seen the article everywhere from the Chicago Tribune and New York Times to the front page of Yahoo, MSN and Fox News.

I also got calls from dozens of complete strangers due to that article. One guy from Tennessee (which is over 1,000 miles away from Oklahoma) left a message on my answering machine wanting to know if I would be interested in driving there to fix his broken Centipede cabinet. Another guy from Dallas called to ask if I would be interested in buying all their old Atari cartridges. But the most interesting call I got because of that article was from a man named Bill Harris, regarding his brother Ed's vintage computer collection.

In the early 1980's, Ed Harris fell in love with the Texas Instruments TI 99/4A personal computer. He bought his first one from a friend who worked directly for Texas Instruments. He loved the machine so much that he bought another. And another. And another. Occasionally Ed would buy TI computers for other people. Bill told me that Ed was so sure his sister would love owning a computer that he bought her a brand new TI 99/4A and had it sent it to her house – along with a bill for it.

For the next twenty years, Ed studied every nook and cranny of those computers. After retirement, Ed spent his days scouring thrift stores and garage sales, looking for Texas Instrument games, programs, and related parts to add to his collection, even if they were duplicates of items he already owned. As stores began to part out their TI inventory, Ed would buy out the entire department. Piles of Texas Instruments hardware filled the corners of his garage.

In 2004, Ed was diagnosed with leukemia and was given three months to live. One of the things Bill and Ed discussed was what to do with Ed's rather large computer collection after his passing. Ed's initial wish was to split the collection up among his grandchildren, but after pitching the idea to them he found that none of them were interested in "those old things." After that, Bill told me Ed had planned on donating the games and computers to either a school or a thrift store, but couldn't find one that would even take his stuff. The two of them even managed to track down former members of a national TI 99/4A user's group, but even *they* didn't want Ed's collection.

Ed's final wish was for Bill and his other family members to simply find someone who would appreciate Ed's retro computer collection, and give it to them.

"And so," Bill said, "after reading your article in the newspaper, we think that you're the guy. Are you interested in the stuff?" he asked.

"Sure!" I said, unable to hide my enthusiasm. "But what's the catch?" I asked.

"No catch," he replied. Bill even agreed to deliver the collection to my house the following day. As it turns out, Bill lived less than ten miles away from me.

True to his word, the following afternoon Bill showed up on my doorstep. He was an older gentleman, probably in his early seventies. After a few minutes of small talk I followed him out to his car to carry in the collection. When I got to the driveway and peeked inside Bill's car, I couldn't believe my eyes. Both the front seat and the rear seat of Bill's sedan were packed with boxes and paper grocery sacks bulging with TI 99/4A stuff. We carried several loads, one after another from the car to the house. And just when I thought the car was empty, Bill informed me that the trunk was full of stuff too. After several more trips, my entire kitchen table was covered in layers of Texas Instruments games, peripherals, hand-written papers, magazines and newsletters, joysticks, speech modules, cassette recorders, wires, and just plain silt. I stood there, dumbfounded, looking at the mound that now covered my entire kitchen table. They say one man's trash is another man's treasure, and I wasn't sure which I had just acquired.

While Bill and I were talking, he told me that whenever his brother would see anything TI 99/4A related in a thrift store or flea market he would pick it up "just in case someone else needed it." I laughed, and then Bill said, "Funny, isn't it?"

"Kind of," I said. "It's funny because I do the exact same thing, just with different stuff. I always kind of feel like it is my responsibility to rescue items from those kinds of places. Every time I see a cheap Atari 2600 I'll buy it with the intention of giving it away to someone who wants one. I have a stack of Sega Genesis consoles just in case someone ever wants one."

"What do the people say when you give them one?" Bill asked.

"That's just it. They never want it. I have half a dozen Commodore 64s sitting out in the garage that I can't give away, and I still buy them because … well, it's kind of hard to explain," I said.

I noticed Bill was looking at me with a comforted but confused smile. I can only assume that Bill had probably heard the same thing from his brother before. I could tell that Bill never quite understood Ed's infatuation with collecting Texas Instruments computers, but I think he began to realize that even though I had never met him, I did.

Whatever he thought, I'm pretty sure he felt that he had found the right guy to pass his brother's collection down to.

I spent the next year giving most of Ed's collection away to fellow collectors. I couldn't bring myself to sell the stuff, and since I never cared much for the TI 99/4A anyway, I'm sure Ed would have preferred his stuff go to people who would have enjoyed it than have it sit collecting dust in my garage. I tried my best to only give things to people who wanted to keep it for their own collection. The only item I kept for myself was Ed's personal Texas Instrument computer; not one of the new ones still sealed in plastic, but the worn out one he regularly used up until he died.

I kind of suspect that Ed was a lot like me. He loved those old computers and he picked them to remind him of those days. That's why I kept one of the computers; to remind me of Ed.

Recently while surfing the web I ran across the Gamebase 64 collection. It's a collection of practically every known Commodore 64 game. The entire collection spans four CDs, and I was able to download it in around an hour's time. Just as a basis of comparison, in the decade I spent collecting Commodore software I amassed around 700 disks of software. Figuring 360k per side and doing a little rounding, it took me around a decade to amass 250 megabytes worth of Commodore 64 games. In sixty minutes I was able to download almost ten times that amount.

I thought that by owning the entire collection I could stop spending my free time in thrift stores, looking for old treasures. Emulation of the C64 on a modern PC is, for all practical purposes, nearly 100% accurate. With just a few mouse clicks I could play any game from my youth. With the addition of a cheap adapter I could even play them using my vintage Commodore 64 joystick!

So why isn't it the same? For the same reason a photocopy of a twenty-dollar bill isn't worth twenty dollars, I suppose. I've listened to argument after argument on the Internet about why emulation isn't the same as the real thing. Some people cite technological reasons: monitor refresh rates, video scaling modes, and all other kinds of high-tech jargon. Personally, I think a lot of it has to do with the way in which the software was acquired. On bulletin boards we were required to trade for software, but on the Internet there's no need to trade with people any more. It's been eliminated. Everything you want is there for the taking. Want every single Commodore 64 game ever made in one nice little package? Click here! Want every Nintendo and Atari 2600 game as well? A few more clicks and you'll have them! There's no hunt any more.

There's no fun in amassing digital archives. When I look at a disk from my old collection it brings back memories. There are no memories downloaded from the Internet. It a completely passive and impersonal task which requires no talent to perform and delivers no enjoyment in return. It would be like collecting photocopies of baseball cards or pictures of bottle caps. The copies have no soul, no spirit. It will never be the same. It's not just the physical item that's different; it's the whole collecting experience that's missing.

I once read about a technique many packrats use that is supposed to make parting with items easier. To make it easier to throw an item away, packrats are advised to first take a picture of it. This allows the person to keep the memory of the item (and any memories associated with it) without having to physically keep the item forever. When I began writing this book, I had an ulterior motive; I had hoped that by transferring all my old BBS memories into the pages of this book, I would finally be able to part with some of my old computer items as well. Unfortunately the exact opposite happened. As I began going through my old computer collection, I found myself as infatuated with it as ever. By going through my collection one last time I found myself as interested as ever in my old stuff.

Last week, during my lunch break I picked up yet another Commodore 1541 disk drive for $5 from a local thrift store. When I saw the drive sitting among other piles of discarded hardware, it was as exciting as the time I found my first one. As I pulled the drive off the shelf and tucked it under my arm, I wasn't thinking about what I was going to do with it; instead, I thought about where it had come from, what its story was. Who knows, maybe it had belonged to someone who I had traded games with once back in the day.

As I ran my fingers across the drive's casing I began to realize that my time spent wandering thrift stores and flea markets wasn't really about the search of stuff at all, but rather the memories those items spark. I'm searching for memories, not games. Each item I pick up and take home takes me back to some great times, even if it's only for a moment.

Although I continue to surround myself with these things that remind me of those days, deep down inside I know that I'll never truly be able to go back. Things will never be the same again.

But it's still fun to remember.

THE BROTHERHOOD OF 405

Yaun-Ti: Married Betite (they met at The Gathering II). They have three or four kids together and live in Norman, Oklahoma.

FalseGod: Married and working for Dell Computers in Austin, Texas.

Buster Friendly: Father to the Phinq, Buster Friendly (also known as Orange1, Leperkhan and Wilhelm Wonka) still delivers pizza in Oklahoma City each night and plays online games each day.

The Stranger: Currently a schoolteacher in the Oklahoma City metro area. The Stranger still writes horror lit for the group Candelabra.

Rivas: Still lives in Oklahoma City and is currently a software project lead for a major avionics company. Rivas describes himself as "happily single."

Gatoperro: Currently working in Bakersfield, California for Haliburton as a Petroleum Field Engineer.

Prong: Moved to Florida and works there as network administrator for a construction company.

Ghost in the Machine: Deceased, 2002.

TDKEB

(T) Violetta Kitten: Has one beautiful daughter and currently attends college. VK is a prolific writer and is currently working on several screenplays and novels.

(D) Deranged: Still lives in the Oklahoma City area, currently works as a DJ, and is about to release her own Mix CD.

(K) Black Sunshine: Recently received her PhD in Sociology and recently relocated to Illinois. Black Sunshine married Mr. Spock, author of the Soulz at Zero viewer.

(E) Anacodia: Became a speech pathologist, married Tekin, and moved to California.

(B) Raven: Moved to England and got married. She currently rides horses, develops websites, and continues to write.

COMMODORE CHARACTERS

Arcane: Currently living in Dallas, Arcane worked as a technical guru for ExxonMobile before they closed their Dallas operations. Arcane currently does computer contracting and consulting in the Dallas area.

Charon: Currently owns his own data warehousing company in Oklahoma City. Met his current wife on the Internet. The two of them now have four children.

Dr. Phrackenstein: Married and currently working as a web designer for the state of Oklahoma.

Klatu: Living in Blanchard, Oklahoma, Klatu still works as a postal carrier and spends very little time on his computer.

MODERN MANIACS

Phosphor Dot Fossils: Founder of TheLogBook.com, one of the most popular sci-fi websites online today. PDF is also an administrator at Digital Press and is the proud parents of many animals ranging from cats to horses.

Icbrkr: Happily married, Icbrkr runs Particles.org and has a huge collection of videogames both old and new.

WHEREABOUTS UNKNOWN

Umbra Sprite, Mister X, The Trooper, Archangel, Bran Mac Morn, 8-Ball, Beetlejuice, Mysteria, Digital Anarchist, Blackcloud, and unfortunately thousands more ...

My Website: http://www.robohara.com

MySpace: http://www.myspace.com/robohara

E-Mail: robohara@robohara.com

TBH405 LiveJournal: http://tbh405.livejournal.com

On IRC: #405 on EfNet

Phosphor Dot Fossils: http://www.thelogbook.com

Icbrkr: http://www.particles.org

Digital Press: http://www.digitpress.com

Cult of the Dead Cow: http://cultdeadcow.com

Jack Flack and The Stranger, Monday Night Raw (2003).